Great Games
to Play with Groups
A Leader's Guide

by Frank W. Harris

Fearon Teacher Aids
Carthage, Illinois

This book is dedicated to the memory of Ruth Norris, my teacher and friend.

Illustrator: Sharyn McDonald, Nevada City, California
Photographers:
Roy Earle, Grand Rapids, Michigan
Sharyn McDonald, Nevada City, California
Fred Newell, Williamsville, New York
Bruce Orwoll, Sunnyvale, California

Contents

Preface

A book is the product of cumulative experience and people, and *Great Games to Play with Groups* is no exception. The seed was planted when the author first tasted the full enjoyment of a cooperative recreation program through a unique group in New York City called Play Co-op. That was in 1939. The seed germinated further when he attended the National Cooperative Recreation School in the Midwest for two consecutive years. There he had the good fortune to be taught games by Neva Boyd of Northwestern University. Her contribution to the author's skills not only increased his repertoire of games but also his understanding of their value and sense of responsibility to game material. The author acknowledges a debt as well to his colleague and friend Ruth Norris, to whom this book is dedicated.

The further development of this book stems from the author's experience for over a quarter century teaching games classes at the Eastern Cooperative Recreation School, a counterpart of the National School. ECRS continues to this day as a vacation workshop for both professionals and nonprofessionals. Its purpose is to teach recreation leadership. Classes are held one to two weeks each summer at different locations in the eastern United States. In addition to games, the school offers courses in folk and square dancing, dramatics, music, crafts, program planning, and practice teaching. Through its classes and social activities, ECRS seeks to help people grow, both as individuals and as members of a group. It presents recreation principles and techniques that can be enjoyed for their own sake and used constructively with others in the community. ECRS is nonprofit and self-supporting. Financed and governed by its members, it is open to all.

The author thanks the following members of ECRS for their help with particular games:

Keith Armstrong for *The Slaves of Job*

Ruth Blaustein for *A-Wuni-Kuni*

Irving Elson for *Play Party Relay*

Sioux Free for *Posture Tag*

Shelley Gordon for *Hands Down 54*

Halina Kantor for *Dzien Dobry*

Ruth Norris for *Broom Croquet, Colored Squares,* and *Plate, Potato, Broom Relay*

Jim Wolfe for *Elephant and Giraffe*

The author owes a debt of gratitude to many others as well who have shared their games and enthusiasm with him:

Neva Boyd for *Capture the Flag, Musical Chairs,* and *Three Deep*

A camper from North Dakota for *Bingo*

Ann Livingston for *Alphabet Race*

Play Co-op, New York, for *How Do You Like Your Neighbor*

Mitsuo Udagawa, National Recreation Association of Japan for *Kendo*

Introduction

Recreation can function as an orientation to life and as an important tool for assisting in the development of an individual toward his or her maximum potential. Games are universal (similar games are played in many countries), and they constitute a recreational skill that can be used anywhere, with any size group, and with little or no equipment. For this reason, games should be included in the repertoire of a recreation leader, school teacher, rehabilitation therapist, child-care staff person, and many others.

Why Games?

From a group leader's point of view, a repertoire of games is not only handy but essential. A leader must be prepared to respond to the many varied situations in which a game is uniquely appropriate. Games can resolve tension, release energy, heal through laughter, enhance self-esteem, promote better group relations, challenge players, develop physical fitness, and heighten problem-solving skills. Good game leaders add to their repertoire constantly. The more games at their command, the more likely they are to fit their knowledge and skill to the needs of a group situation.

Who Plays Games?

Frequently, adults respond to the subject by saying, "Games are for children." Not so. Games are for people, including children. The majority of games in this collection can be played and enjoyed by everyone over the age of 6. Youngsters respond to games in fairly uninhibited fashion. Teenagers sometimes adopt a veneer of sophistication and try to copy adults, rejecting games as childish. They can be reached, however, and they'll play—with verve. Adults are even easier, requiring little encouragement. The proper choice of a game at the right moment is usually all that is needed to set the stage for a few hours of genuine fun, participation, and group spirit.

The games in this book can be played by male and female alike; however, in order to avoid the grammatical encumbrance of "he or she" in describing game moves, I have alternated genders throughout the book. The age levels for playing the games are indicated as 6 and up, 7 and up, and so forth. "And up" means all ages through seniors, although a general rule should be applied with care. For instance, players who are less agile, slightly handi-capped, or concerned about roughness must be considered in determining the appropriateness of a particular game. *Quick Line-up,* although an excellent game for most ages, might not work well with people over 60 who are less sprightly. Then, too, if a few of the members are physically handicapped but quite able to play many of the games, it is not necessary to limit all participants to only those games that the handicapped can play. I choose instead to recognize that a few players are handicapped and inform them directly that some of the games will not be appropriate for them.

A Concept of Game Play

When leading a game workshop, my basic philosophy is expressed in a sentence: "Laughter should be with, not at, and no one should be made to feel inept, inadequate, or incompetent in a game situation." In other words, laughter should be free and uninhibited, not directed at a specific person or persons. No one should be made to feel uncom-fortable, singled out, or embarrassed. Everyone should find his or her own niche in the game. The participants' enjoy-ment will be the only motivation they need to improve their level of play.

Group Relations

Games can help whether you are working with a group of strangers who are having difficulty relaxing and being themselves, or with a group that feels ill at ease because of differences of race, nationality, or religion. A half hour of games can dissolve the feelings of estrangement and produce a climate of friendliness, acceptance, and fun.

Games in which there is considerable interchange of players, abundant physical contact, and frequent, vigorous movement are appropriate for such situations. They are commonly known as "mixers," "warmer-uppers," or "ice-breakers." Many are included in this book, and more can be found in other books on games. But be wary of getting-acquainted gimmicks. Some are so artificial and strained that they serve only to accentuate feelings of discomfort and strangeness. An example is an activity called *Car Wash*. The activity (it is not a game) consists of people kneeling in two lines while one player crawls from one end of the line to the other, in effect running the gauntlet. Each player in line touches the person, simulating windshield washers, washing the underside of a car, washing the top, washing the windows. For some people, this touching can become decidedly uncomfortable.

Problem Solving

No matter how simple a game may be, it presents a problem to be solved by the players. A leader who gives the problem-solving element free rein permits the game to spark creativity, imagination, active interest, and maximum group interaction. The leader who does not, reduces the players to robots. If players are to grow from playing a game, they must be permitted to test themselves, both as individuals and through interaction with the other players. The leader's job is to give the essential rules to get the game going. The player's job is to play.

Don't give in to the impulse to share with the players your knowledge of the fine points of a game. The bare skeleton of the game is enough. Leave it to them to put the flesh on the bones. As long as they enjoy the game, it will present a challenge to them. They will add their knowledge of how to play and enjoy the satisfaction that comes with knowing they developed the skill themselves. For example, *Snatch the Bacon* requires two players, one from each team, to rush forward. One picks up the object from the floor midway between the two teams and attempts to run with it back to her place in line before being tagged by the opposing player. Two points are scored by the player making it back without being tagged. One point is scored by the player who succeeds in tagging the runner with the "bacon" before the runner reaches safety in line.

If just the rules are taught, the leader will find players rushing out pell mell, grabbing the object immediately, and rushing back to the line. The advantage is always with the player who does not have to pick up the object, since all that player has to do is continue in one direction to tag the opponent. The latter must reverse direction in order to make it back.

Depending upon the age of the group or the number of players who have played the game before, this pattern of play may go on for a long time. In my experience with a group of 8- and 9-year-olds, the children played the game several times this way before they discovered it made more sense to stop at the object and try to feint the other player out of position before picking it up. But they found out for themselves! They solved the problem. Don't become impatient and give in to the temptation to help the group solve the problem.

Competition—Yea or Nay?

About half the games in this book can be described as "cooperative" or "win-win" for all participants. The team games, however, involve dividing into teams, keeping score, and eventually one side becoming a winner.

Competition is not bad per se. If winning is incidental to the fun of playing, then competition can intensify the game, and players will feel comfortable regardless of their level of ability. But if a person's primary motivation is to win, that motivation is often destructive, leading to unde-sirable shortcuts in playing the game and, frequently, to derision directed at a teammate who makes an error or is not as quick as the others. There are a few things that one can and should do to lessen the importance of winning and enhance interest in the playing of the game.

1. *Choose teams randomly.* One way is to have the players count off. If two teams are needed, they count off one-two, one-two. If three or more teams are needed, they count off in threes, fours, and so forth. When teams do not have to be exactly the same number, try dividing the group according to month of birth.

   A pattern that fortunately is disappearing from our schools and playgrounds—selecting captains who in turn choose the teams—is extremely damaging to people. Those individuals who are chosen last, next to last, next to next to last, and so on down the line, feel inferior, hurt, and ultimately become the ones who avoid games. When playing with adults, it is interesting to ask them how many were chosen first as children and how many were chosen last. Most of the hands are raised in response to the latter.

2. *Set the winning score during the playing of the game, not at the beginning.* Instruct the teams to keep track of their scores, but don't tell them what score will win until later in the game. Then, ask how many points each team has, and based on when you want the game to end, set a winning score. Groups recognize quickly that the winning score is really determined by your time clock, even though the winning team is acknowledged when the game ends.

3. *Change teams for each game.* Even if the same number of team members is needed for the game that follows, select random teams once again. This avoids the pitfalls that can occur in identifying with one group of players.

If winning does not dominate, competition can be constructive and provide an edge, an excitement, to playing games. Games like *Scavenger Hunt* or *Bird, Beast, or Fish* generate a competitive spirit each time players from the different teams come out to the center to learn what they are to do. The excitement is in the scoring of individual team points. When teams are asked how many points they have, and they answer with absurdly high scores, I know the final outcome no longer is important to them. Simply winning each point is what counts. It is then that competition is of greatest value to the players.

Elimination Games, Good or Bad?

Many games in game collections include the elimination element. Sometimes this means that the first to be eliminated from the game are those who are slow in catching on or in coordinating physical and mental reactions. As the game nears completion, almost everyone has been eliminated and the contest is reduced to a battle between the last two supposedly "best" players. Meanwhile, those who are now on the sidelines may be losing interest in the contest, creating distractions, or wandering off. Fragmenting of focus almost always results when elimination of players is not essential to the playing of the game.

If a game in this book demands elimination in order to be played, players are eliminated almost completely by chance. Thus they are unlikely to feel less skillful than others. Also, the game still holds their interest, since it is amusing to watch. As a game leader acquiring a repertoire, ask yourself two questions: Can the game be played only with elimination, and if so, is the game fun to watch? If the answer to both these questions is yes, then the game is a true elimination game and runs little or no risk of embarrassing anyone. If the answer to the first question is no, the elimination element can be replaced with a positive goal. In this collection, *Reverse Buzz* is an example of a game in which the positive goal of reaching 50 replaces elimination. *Last Couple Stoop* is an example of a game in which elimination is an integral part of the game.

Tricks, Stunts, Novelties

If our purpose in recreation is to avoid singling out an individual in a way that makes the person feel conspicuous, inferior, or unwanted, how do we justify many of the tricks and stunts that abound at parties? There are many acceptable tricks and stunts in which the players participate voluntarily, with full knowledge of what is required. These are situations in which all participants face the same handicap rather than some of the group being "in the know" and some not. *Drawing in the Dark* is an example of a novelty in which all players start with the same handicap, and, as with all tricks, stunts, or novelties, once played it cannot be played again. The element of surprise or the solution to the trick is the key factor.

Tricks or stunts that single out certain people and place a premium upon their not knowing in advance what they are in for almost invariably make them the "butt" or the "scapegoat." There is no place for this type of activity in a good recreation program. The "blindfold-egg" stunt, although seemingly innocuous, is a good example. Volunteers are told they will have to walk blindfolded across a floor strewn with fresh eggs. The players are shown the irregular pattern of eggs on the floor and told to memorize the egg positions. Then the players are blind-folded and the eggs removed from the floor. To the ex-cruciating mirth of the onlookers, the players step gingerly over nonexistent eggs. Harmless? Perhaps. But if just one player in the blindfolded group feels foolish or inferior for not knowing this stunt, then the stunt is unnec-essary and does not contribute to that player's feeling part of the group. It serves instead to make the player uncom-fortable and removes her further from a sense of belonging. The player is laughed at, not with.

Dramatic Games

Dramatic games merit special comment. Many teenagers and adults are loathe to place themselves in an acting situation. They may be worried about what others will think. They may be afraid of appearing silly. This type of inhibition shows up in other games, too, but does not affect the playing of the game as drastically as it does in dramatic games that depend upon a player's feeling free to "act."

The dramatic games in this book provide the freest kind of opportunity for the player to be relaxed while playing, because the readiness to act is left to each player to determine. Despite this, the caution still holds that if group members are not at ease with each other, dramatic games are not good program starters.

Used appropriately, dramatic games not only provide an enjoyable and satisfying experience, they also serve as an introduction to more disciplined forms of dramatics. For the leader interested in helping a group move from acting small scenes without memorizing lines to play production and creative dramatics, the following progression of dramatic games is recommended: *Bird, Beast, or Fish; I'm Thinking of a Word That Rhymes With; The Game; Anagram Charades.*

Game Leadership

In summation, several points should be emphasized with respect to teaching games.

1. *Be prepared with a list of games to be played and the necessary equipment.* Know the approximate number of players you will have, the type of playing area, and what games you want to teach. Gather whatever equipment is needed and bring it with you. But be flexible. Be prepared to adjust the list of games based on the group's needs.

2. *Start positively.* If you think a game fits the situation, you might say, "Everyone up in a circle for *Three Deep.*" Don't ask, "Does anyone want to play a game?" There are two answers to that question, and you are just as likely to get a no as a yes. Rely on your own judgment.

3. *Get the group in position to play before explaining the rules.* If a game is played in line formation with two teams, have the group count off by twos and line up.

4. *Make instructions brief.* Don't talk a group to death nor intellectualize the rules. Give just enough of the rules to get the game going. Don't try to anticipate all situations that can occur. There will be time enough to provide additional rules if the situations requiring the rules arise.

5. *Demonstrate or do a dry run.* Certain games, such as *Scavenger Hunt, Quick Line-up,* and *Snatch the Bacon,* lend themselves to a dry run for practice. Other games are more easily taught when the leader demonstrates,

such as *Face to Face* and *Three Deep*. Remember, if you are demonstrating as the leader and are playing, you still need to settle issues if they arise and make additional rules if required. You also must decide when to end the game.

6. *End a game before it reaches a peak of enjoyment.* Enjoyment in playing a game resembles a bell curve. It rises, reaches a peak, and then falls. Stopping the game just before the peak or at the peak is advisable. Most games are fun to play over and over again, always offering new challenges to the players. Play a game too long, and you may kill the fun and the group's interest in playing it again.

7. *Delay setting the winning score.* In all the games in this book where one team scores points against another, it is not necessary to set a winning score before the game starts. Just ask each team to keep track of its own scores. If there are two teams, the leader can keep the score. Play for a while, check each team's score once or twice, and then announce what the winning score will be. That score will be based upon how well the game is going and when you think the game should end. Be sure to acknowledge the winning team before moving on to the next game.

8. *Reach for lasting results.* Leadership training should strive to provide a sound philosophy based on the importance of the individual and skills that are tools for personal growth. The game is not an end in itself, but it does have a purpose: to provide a fun experience and a sense of satisfaction and achievement. The development of the players' skills must come from within, from their own motivation, which in turn contributes to their growth as human beings. A good leader knows not only how to teach games but also what each game has to offer to the group and to the individual participants.

Index According to Number of Players

Note: The indicated number of players is only a guide; use it flexibly.

Index According to Level of Physical Activity

Index According to Type of Game*

*Some games fall into more than one type.

The Games

ALPHABET RACE

Indoor   ***20–40 Players***

To enjoy this game, all you need to know is how to spell. Everyone coaches everyone else, confusion reigns, and team spirit takes hold. This game is excellent for mixed-age groups. Teachers can make spelling fun, adjusting the words to the pupils' grade level.

Equipment
Two sets of alphabet cards, 6" x 6" cardboard, each with a letter of the alphabet printed large enough to see from a distance. Two tables to hold each set of cards spread out face up.

Formation
Two teams lined up in columns. A table is placed 20 to 25 feet in front of the first player in each team.

Action
The leader calls out a word. From the beginning of each line, enough players to spell the word run to the table, find their letters, and face their teams, letters held in front of them. The word must be spelled correctly and read properly from the vantage point of the teams and the leader. First side to complete the word scores a point for their team. Players who have just formed a word place their letters back on the table, face up, and return to the end of their line.

The leader must enunciate clearly and avoid words that use a letter more than once. Words like the following are good: *stormy, country, guitar, scramble, friends, pencil, social, juices, education, parties, hysterical, eight, drawing.*

The leader should scramble the letters on the tables frequently, since team members inevitably attempt to separate them to make it more convenient for the next player. No harm is done if some cards lie partly on others.

Play long enough to give each player several chances.

Variation
One person at a time runs to the table, finds the correct letter, turns, and faces teammates before the next player runs up to find a letter. This is more orderly and less confusing and may be desirable in some situations.

ANAGRAM CHARADES

Anagram Charades is a dramatic game that takes time to play but is well worth it. Mixed groups from age 8 up can play, including parents and grandparents. Players determine their own parts in the charade. Parts may range from the Queen of Sheba to a bathroom faucet or a giraffe. For maximum benefit from this game, play it after the group has had several good experiences resulting in relaxation and a sense of belonging. Allow at least 45 minutes to play.

Equipment
Small squares of paper, on each of which a number and one letter of a word has been written. For example, if the first word to be dramatized is *earthquake,* each letter of that word is written on a separate slip of paper together with the number 1. Each letter of the next word is written with the numeral 2, and so forth.

Words used for this game should consist of two parts, each with dramatic potential, for example:

earthquake	makeshift	spellbound	anteater
rainfall	killjoy	grab bag	bedbug
Shakespeare	ice cream	earthworm	crab meat
warfare	snake bite	claptrap	mess call

Formation
None. The players assemble en masse to hear the instructions. They divide into groups whose size depends on the number of letters in each of the words. Extra players can be divided equally among the groups.

The area in which the game is played should permit groups to rehearse without interfering with each other. Ideally, there should be a few separate rooms in which this can be done. The groups come back together at a specified time or at the direction of the leader.

Action
The slips of paper are placed in a hat in the center of the room, and the leader mixes them up. Each player selects a slip and joins other players with the same numbered slip. Leftover slips are distributed to the numbered groups by the leader. If there are too few papers, the extra players can be assigned to groups. As soon as players find their team, they unscramble their word. Then the team prepares a charade to dramatize the word.

Groups are encouraged to develop scenes based upon the parts of the word and on the word as a whole. They may use pantomime, dramatization with words and props, or tableaus (for example, they can rehearse a scene, bring it to a peak, and freeze at that point into a tableau, presenting only the tableau to the audience). Props may be human, with a player portraying an inanimate object.

The key to dramatic presentations is for each scene to have a beginning, a middle, and an end. Although rehearsed only briefly, each scene should tell a story, hang together. The audience must not try to guess what the word is until all scenes have been acted.

If possible, each team should include a person who has participated before in this type of informal charade and who can provide limited direction. This person should ensure that each member of the team has an opportunity to share in creating the story and selecting a role for each scene, rather than having a role imposed by an overeager player who is full of ideas and will tell everyone who they are to be and how they are to act.

The group is also advised at the start of the game that it will have a certain amount of time to prepare the dramatizations. At the end of that time, the groups will reassemble, and then each team in turn will present its scenes to the others.

It is important to complete all instructions before the players select slips and separate into groups. From that point on, they proceed without interruption. The leader should circulate among all groups, in case any are having trouble figuring out what the word is or spending too much time in deciding upon a story.

A-WUNI-KUNI

Indoor or Outdoor   *Any Number of Players*

This chant is good with any group from the age of 5 on, including mixed-age groups. At the end of a game session, the chant has a unifying effect.

A Wu-ni Ku-ni Kai-ai Wu-ni   Kai-ai - ai yi - pi

Ai Kai-yay-kis.   A wu.   A Wu-ni Ki-chi.

Equipment
None.

Formation
Players sit on floor or in chairs in a circle, close enough so that they can easily reach the next person.

Action
All movements are done in time to the chant, with the first movement beginning on the syllable *wu*.

- Movement 1—Both hands on own knees. Move both hands simultaneously one knee to the right, so that one's right hand is on neighbor's left knee and one's left hand on one's own right knee. Then repeat to left. Repeat to end of chant. Movement ends with hands on self only.
- Movement 2—Begin with hands on own knees, cross hands on own knees, uncross on own knees. Then extend hands, placing one hand on the nearest knee of each neighbor. Repeat to end of chant.
- Movement 3—Same as Movement 2, except that hands start at chest and, on movement to right and left, players touch palms with neighbors. Repeat to end of chant.
- Movement 4—Extend left arm forward. On first beat touch right hand to left wrist. On second beat touch right hand to upper arm. On third beat fold arms over chest. On fourth beat extend right arm. Repeat with left hand. Repeat to end of chant.
- Movement 5—Tap floor with hands. Then tap chest, tap side of head, raise hands to sky, then tap chest again. (Note that you do not touch side of head on way back to chest.) Repeat to end of chant.

As group becomes more proficient with chant and with movements, the tempo is increased.

BATTLESHIP

Indoor   ***2–3 Players***

Even though this game has gone commercial with prepared "oceans"
ready for the players, I find it a wonderfully challenging game for a quiet
time. Rumor has it that Lord Nelson played this game when plotting naval
strategy for the Battle of Trafalgar. Whether or not this is true, young and
old will enjoy pitting their wits against each other in an effort to "sink" the
other player's fleet. Recommended for ages 7 and up.

Equipment
Paper and pencils. Graph paper with large boxes (at least $1/4$") speeds up
the outlining of "oceans" and the disposition of "fleets."

Formation
Players sit at a table or on couches or cushions—anything comfortable.
They need only a firm base on which to place their paper.

Action
On his paper each player outlines two oceans. Each ocean has ten boxes
across and ten boxes down. Across the top of each ocean, each column is
headed by a letter of the alphabet, A through J. Down the left-hand side
each column is numbered 1 through 10.

On the same paper each player makes a chart of his fleet: a battleship
is five boxes, a cruiser is four, a destroyer is three, and two submarines
are two boxes each. The chart of the fleet is needed in order to keep
track of the hits on the other fleet.

Each player outlines his fleet in one of his two oceans. (See
illustration.) The ships may be outlined horizontally or vertically. No more
than one box of any ship may touch the outside rows of boxes. No ship
may touch more than one box of another ship. The players must conceal
their fleets from each other.

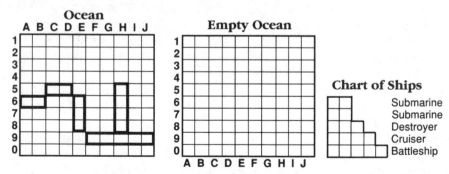

If two are playing, the game commences with each player in turn
firing a salvo at the opposing player. If three are playing, the salvo is fired
at the player to the left.

A salvo consists of five shots. A shot is identified by citing the letter and number of the box to be hit, for example, B-3. The player firing his first salvo enters a 1 in the appropriate box of his empty ocean for each shot in the salvo. The player fired at enters a 1 in the appropriate box in the ocean in which he has outlined his fleet. On the conclusion of a salvo, both players have five 1s entered in their oceans.

After the salvo of five shots, the player fired at informs the other player whether any shot hit a ship. All that he reveals, however, is, "You got a shot in my destroyer," or "You got one hit in my cruiser," or "All the shots were in the ocean." He must not identify exactly which shot hit which ship.

If any ships were hit, the player who fired the salvo enters a 1 in a box of the appropriate ship on his chart of ships. He also records each shot in the salvo with a 1 in the appropriate boxes in his empty ocean.

By keeping track of the hits scored, each player is attempting to locate the enemy fleet. After a player has hit all the boxes of an enemy ship, that ship is sunk and the player is so informed at the end of the salvo. For each ship sunk, the player sinking the ship loses one shot in his salvo.

The winner is the player who not only sinks all the ships of another player but also outlines that player's fleet correctly in his empty ocean.

Variations

The player whose ship is sunk, rather than the player sinking the ship, loses a shot in his salvo.

Some versions of the game permit a ship to be outlined diagonally. Other versions also allow more than one box to touch the outside border as well as other ships.

BECKON

Outdoor   *14–30 Players*

A variation of *Hide and Seek,* this game combines the fun of hiding with the excitement of capture and the thrill of escape. The game is also known as *Sheep in My Pen.* It suits children from the age of 6, as well as mixed-age groups.

Equipment

None.

Formation

The selection of playing area is most important to this game. A small, clearly defined area in which the players can all stand is designated as the prison. It must be located in a semi-exposed area so that it is neither too easy nor too difficult to flee and find a hiding place. The total area for playing should provide many hiding places from which players can see the prison. Players are not permitted to go into buildings.

Action

One person is "it." While standing at the prison, "it" hides his eyes and counts to 100, giving the others time to find hiding places. The players scatter and find hiding places, making sure the prison is within view.

On finishing the count, "it" looks for other players. Upon sighting one, "it" identifies the player by name or by clothing and states exactly where the player is hiding. The player then walks to the prison unaccompanied.

As soon as a captured player is in prison, she loudly calls for a "beckon." Any free player can give her a beckon by beckoning with a finger and being seen by the prisoner. When a prisoner has a beckon, she can leave the prison at any time. If she succeeds in fleeing the prison and finds another hiding place without being seen by "it," she is free to give beckons to other players. If "it" sees her escaping and identifies her, she must return to prison. To try to escape again, she must call for and get another beckon.

"It" tries to capture all the players, finding those still hidden while at the same time keeping the captured players in prison. The game ends when "it" has all players in prison.

If there are too many players, two players can be "it."

THE BIG WIND BLOWS

Indoor   *15–40 Players*

Similar to *How Do You Like Your Neighbor?* this game affords opportunities for creative thinking and ensures considerable movement through changing of seats. The resulting scramble makes the game a good icebreaker. Mixed-age groups from 7 up can play.

Equipment

Individual chairs without arms. One less chair than players.

Formation

All players except the leader, who has no chair, sit in a large circle—the more space the better.

Action

The leader says, "The big wind blows all those who . . . ," adding an action that some or all in the group may have done or are doing now, for example: brushed their teeth last night, dressed this morning, are wearing eyeglasses, aren't wearing socks. All players whom the statement fits rise and find another seat. In the scramble, the leader finds a chair. The player left without a chair becomes the next leader.

Note

Persons sitting next to empty chairs should, to the extent possible, reach out and hold the chairs firm as players scramble to find seats.

BINGO

Indoor   *20 or More Players*

This singing game is simple and fun for any group from age 8 up. It is particularly successful when performed at the end of a group's experience at a camp, school, or institute. Such dances were popular with the early settlers and pioneers.

Equipment

Piano and pianist, or the singing of the dancers.

Formation

Circle with partners

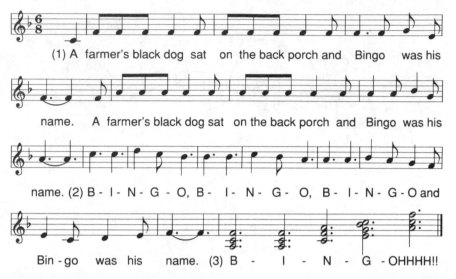

(1) A farmer's black dog sat on the back porch and Bingo was his name. A farmer's black dog sat on the back porch and Bingo was his name. (2) B - I - N - G - O, B - I - N - G - O, B - I - N - G - O and Bin - go was his name. (3) B - I - N - G - OHHHH!!

Action

Couples hold hands in promenade or skating position (right hand holding right hand, left hand holding left hand, arms crossed in front), facing counterclockwise.

1. Couples promenade in counterclockwise direction.
2. Turn in place and promenade in opposite direction.
3. Couples face each other. Boys will promenade in counterclockwise direction, and girls will continue in clockwise direction. Begin grand right and left, commencing with right hand to partner on the letter *B*, then left hand to next girl on *I*, and so on until the end of the word. On "OHHHH," the boy shakes the girl's hand enthusiastically. (If the players are older, the man can pick up and hug his partner, if so inclined.)

The first verse resumes and the dance starts over. The boy's new partner is the girl he reached on "OHHHH!"

   If a pianist is playing, he should resume playing promptly after the "OHHHH!" If the group is singing the words as they dance, the leader signals the start of the next repeat of the dance by singing out loudly.

BIRD, BEAST, OR FISH

Indoor   *20 or More Players*

Popular with any group above the age of 6, this game can serve both as a mixer and as an introduction to dramatic games. When used with a group of strangers, the acting will be more inhibited, but the game will generate enthusiasm nevertheless. The greatest potential of this game can be achieved when people are more at ease with each other or when used with a group that has been together more than once. See *Quick Line-up, Face to Face,* or *Scavenger Hunt* as good warmer-uppers before using this game.

Equipment
None.

Formation
Players are divided into teams, each team not exceeding ten players. The number of teams depends upon the size of the group and the size of the room. The teams are dispersed to the corners and sides of the room with the leader taking a position in the center, equidistant from each team.

Action
Teams send one player each to the leader, who whispers to them the name of a bird, beast, or fish: for example, *elephant.* The players hear the word at the same time and then run back to their teams to act out *elephant* in pantomime. No sounds are used. As soon as a team member guesses *elephant,* the player who is acting runs back and touches the leader, repeating *elephant.* The first player back to the leader scores a point for his team.

Teammates may ask the acting players questions, and they may nod their heads to answer. The acting players may also indicate in pantomime that a team member is hot or cold. The exact "bird, beast, or fish" must be named by the team.

Set a winning score after the game starts, and base that score on how well the game is going.

BRONCO TAG

Indoor or Outdoor   ***14–30 Players***

Active, rough, and exciting, this game is recommended for teenagers and young adults. Although it can be played coed, sanity dictates that the game be played by all males or all females.

Equipment
None.

Formation
An unobstructed indoor or outdoor area, large enough for running in and out. Pairs of players form a circle. One player stands behind the other, grasping the latter around the waist.

Action
Two players are not joined. One is the chaser and the other tries to escape. "It" is the one doing the chasing. The player trying to escape attempts to maneuver himself into position in front of a pair, or bronco, so that the front end of the bronco can grasp and hold on to him around the waist. If he succeeds, he is safe, and the rear end of the bronco must flee, with "it" pursuing him. If the chaser tags the player trying to escape, they reverse roles.

   In this game the front end of the bronco always tries to grasp the fleeing player. The rear person always tries to keep the front end from succeeding. He may physically swing the front end any way he wishes to accomplish this.

BROOM CROQUET (GERMAN)

Indoor   ***20–40 Players***

Although hard on the brooms, this game is exciting and loads of fun to play. If you can find a push broom that absolutely will not break during the game, you are doing well. Eight-year-olds and up, both genders, can play, but care should be taken to match fairly evenly players who will oppose each other. This can be done in part by having each team line up according to height.

Equipment
Two strong push brooms, two chairs, and a rag.

Formation
A small gym or game room is fine. The size of the room will depend on the number of players. Players divide into two teams and line up against opposite walls facing each other. Players number off, starting at the right-hand end of their line. (Number 1s are therefore at diagonally opposite ends of the room.) One chair is placed at each end of the room, midway between the two teams. A push broom is placed on the floor in front of each chair, with the brush end toward the chair and the handle parallel to the team that guards it. The rag is placed midway between the chairs and at an equal distance from each side.

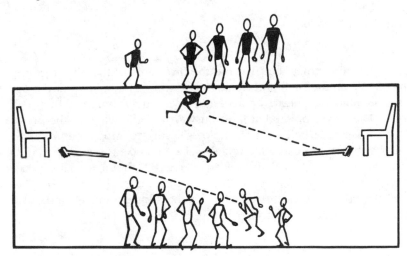

Action
The leader calls any number in the line. Both players whose number is called run and pick up the broom identified as belonging to their team.

The two players then try to push the rag between the legs of the opposing team's chair. The first player to succeed scores a point for his team.

After scoring a point, the brooms are replaced next to the appropriate chairs, the rag is put back in the center, and the leader calls another number. The game continues until most of the players, if not all, have had at least one chance—or until you run out of brooms.

BUMPETY-BUMP-BUMP

Indoor   *15–25 Players*

Many gimmicks have been created by those who attach great importance to being able to assign a name to a face. Parties abound with novelties designed to introduce one person to another. Here is a game that does it naturally, with no fuss or feather.

Equipment
Chairs.

Formation
Players sit in a circle.

Action
All players are instructed to find out the first name of the player sitting immediately on their left and right. One player in the middle of the circle is "it." "It" points at a seated player and says, "Right, bumpety-bump-bump." The player pointed at must answer with the name of the person seated on her right before "it" completes saying "bumpety-bump-bump."

If the player succeeds, she remains seated, and "it" continues to point to players, varying "right" and "left" as desired. If the player fails to say the name in time or responds with the wrong name, she takes the place of "it." An "it" who unseats a player must be allowed time to find out the names of the people next to her before being challenged.

CALL BALL

Outdoor or Indoor   ***10–20 Players***

This game is lively good fun and better outdoors than in, although indoors is satisfactory if the space is large enough and the ceiling high enough.

Equipment

A volleyball that is not inflated too hard, or any lightweight ball of the same size. A sponge ball can be used.

Formation

Players group loosely around the first person to throw the ball up in the air.

Action

All players number off consecutively. One player starts the game by throwing the ball straight up in the air. At the same time, he calls out any number except his own. The player whose number was called tries to catch the ball before it hits the ground. All the other players run away from the ball. If the player catches the ball, he can immediately throw it up again and call another number.

If the ball hits the ground before he retrieves it, he calls "stop." All players then freeze where they are. The player with the ball takes three steps toward any player and rolls or throws the ball at him. The player at whom the ball is directed cannot move. If he is hit, a point is charged against him. Each player can accumulate a maximum of three points against him. (This number is arbitrary and can be changed to a higher total, particularly if the number of players is small.)

The player who threw the ball is the next player to throw the ball in the air and call another number.

Note

Although a player is eliminated if he gets the total number of points, the fun of the game is the playing and not the elimination. Setting five points as the total that can be accumulated should result in a game ending before any players are eliminated.

CAPTURE THE FLAG

Outdoor or Indoor   ***20–30 Players***

As a game that offers an opportunity for innumerable strategies combined with physical pushing and pulling, *Capture the Flag* is played all over the country under many names. When playing outdoors, players may be pulled along the ground, resulting in grass stains. When playing indoors on a wooden floor, wood burns may result. Players should be cautioned about these possibilities. Eight-year-olds and up enjoy this game.

Equipment
Two flags (handkerchiefs).

Formation
A well-marked playing area with clearly defined boundaries and a center dividing line. The size of the area depends upon the number of players. A flag is placed at the rear center, preferably about 5 to 6 feet high. A prison area is marked off at the diagonally opposite corners of each team's playing area. The prison box should be about 3 feet square.

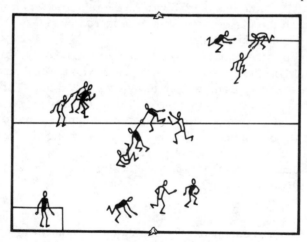

Action
Players are divided into two teams. Teams develop their own strategies with respect to prisoners and the flag. The main object of the game is to steal the opponent's flag without being caught. Another objective is to capture as many prisoners as possible.

A member of the opposing team is caught when she has both feet in the enemy territory, and a player from that side has both hands on her. Once a player is caught, she proceeds, without guard, to the prison.

Players may be pulled, pushed, or moved in almost any other way in order to get them across the center line. Players can form a chain into the other side's territory as long as the last player on the chain has one foot in her own territory. Similarly, prisoners may form a chain as long as the last prisoner caught has one foot in the prison. They must form their chain in the order they were caught. The chain cannot extend across the center line.

A prisoner is freed when touched by an uncaught player from her side who has both feet in the enemy territory. Once freed, the prisoner and the person freeing return to their own side. They cannot be captured.

When the flag is stolen, the teams return to their own side. The number of times the flag may be stolen depends upon the level of interest and excitement. A point is scored each time a flag is stolen.

Variation

Another version of the game is called *Picking Up Sticks*. The rules are basically the same, except that instead of two flags, a small pile of sticks is placed at the rear center of each team's area. The object is to steal one stick at a time. The team that succeeds in stealing all of its opponent's sticks wins.

CAT AND DOG

Indoor or Outdoor   ***15–25 Players***

Young and old can play this game but not as a mixed group. It is not advisable to mix 8- to 12-year-olds with adults. Teenagers and adults do well together. Complete madness may be the result, but don't let it stop you. Seeing is believing. It can be done.

Equipment
Chairs or benches.

Formation
Players sit close together in a circle.

Action
The leader offers a small object, identified as a "dog," to the player on his right. At the same time he says, "I give you a dog." The player to whom it is offered asks, "A what?" The leader replies, "A dog." Then, and only then, is the object passed to the player. She, in turn, repeats the ritual with the player on her right. When she is asked, "A what?" she turns and asks the leader, "A what?" The leader then replies, "A dog," and this phrase is passed back. Each time the question must be passed all the way back to the leader, and the leader's response must be passed all the way back to the person offering the object.

Simultaneously, the leader starts the other object to his left by saying, "I give you a cat." The player on his left then asks, "A what?" and the same routine is then continued.

The goal of the game is to see which object, the dog or the cat, can travel around the complete circle first. The high point in the game is when the dog and cat cross each other somewhere about the middle of the circle. Although the game may appear to be disintegrating into chaos, stay with it! Everyone will be frantically calling questions and answers.

CHAIN PANTOMIME

Indoor or Outdoor   ***5 Players Plus Spectators***
This novelty game combines dramatic opportunity and mirth. Be sure the game is explained fully before asking for volunteers. No one should be placed in an acting situation who does not wish to be. Willingness is essential in this game.

Equipment
None.

Formation
Except for the actors, the rest of the group is the audience and should be seated in a semicircle so that acting can take place at the open end.

Action
Five volunteers leave the room or step out of earshot. While they are gone, the group determines a specific action to be pantomimed in detail, for example, changing a flat tire. One member of the group agrees to pantomime the idea. Whoever agrees should be sure to perform a series of connected actions as clearly as possible.

When the action has been agreed upon and demonstrated, one of the five volunteers is called back to the group, the other four remaining out of sight. The action is pantomimed for the volunteer who, in turn, attempts to repeat the pantomime for the next volunteer called back. This volunteer repeats the pantomime for the next volunteer, and so on until the fifth volunteer has returned and had the opportunity to watch the action. This last volunteer then tries to guess what the original action was.

By this time, naturally, the action has undergone many changes. At the end, it is interesting to find out what each person was trying to do and then to demonstrate the original action for the benefit of those who were out of the room.

COLORED SQUARES (GERMAN)

Indoor   ***2 Players Plus Spectators***

The idea of finding out what a person has pinned to his back is common to many countries. This version comes from Germany. It can be useful during a break in activities at a party, in the classroom, or on a playground. As for all novelty games, it is essential to let the prospective players know what is in store for them before asking for volunteers.

Equipment
Four to six 2" squares of paper, each square a different color, plus two straight pins.

Formation
None, other than sufficient space for two people to maneuver around each other. Nonplayers should be able to hear and watch the action.

Action
The two volunteers face away from the leader as a colored square is pinned on each one's back between the shoulder blades. Neither player knows the color on his back or on his opponent's. The leader then turns the two so they face each other, being careful to keep the colors hidden from the players.

The players shake hands and introduce themselves. Then, keeping their hands behind their backs so that they cannot push or turn the other player, they carry on a continuous conversation while moving around. Each player attempts to identify the color of the square on his opponent's back. The first one to name the color correctly wins. Guessing is not permitted. The player must see the colored square.

This game can be played as long as there are willing volunteers.

COME ALONG

Indoor   ***14–30 Players***

This game can be a good mixer. Players should be encouraged to take the hand that is offered to them, although they may remain seated if they wish, *Come Along* is good for all ages from 6 up, including mixed-age groups.

Equipment

One less chair than the number of players and a record player or a piano and piano player (if the teacher or a group member is not enlisted to sing).

Formation

Players sit in a circle.

Action

One player is the leader. While music is played or the teacher or a nonplayer sings, the leader walks around the inside of the circle extending a hand. The seated players choose whether to take the hand or not. When a seated player takes the proffered hand and joins the leader, that player extends the other hand to the seated players. More and more players join the group walking around the inside of the circle.

When the music or singing stops, all players rush for a seat. The player left without a seat starts the game again.

CROWS AND CRANES

Outdoor or Indoor   ***20–40 Players***

This seemingly pointless game generates competition between the sides, no matter which side you happen to end up on. Children from 8 through 12 get a great kick out of trying to anticipate the leader's call. Teens accustomed to playing games will like this. It is excellent for family groups, provided none of the family members are on the aging side.

Equipment

None.

Formation

Two lines of about the same number of players stand 3 feet apart, facing each other. If played indoors, a large unobstructed room is required, preferably a gym. The two lines stand in the middle of the floor, with the wall on either side serving as the point to which the team runs. The distance from each team to the wall should be about 30 feet. If played outdoors, an unobstructed area is required, plus a line behind which a player is "safe." The distance must be the same for both teams.

Action

The leader stands at the end and between the two lines. One team is designated as the Crows and the other as the Cranes. The players are instructed that whenever their team's name is called, they are to run to the wall or to some point designated behind them. The other team will chase them. Once the game starts, Crows must run whenever the leader says "Crows," and Cranes must chase them, and vice versa.

Members of the chasing team capture players by touching them. Chasing players may touch as many running players as they can before the runners reach safety—the wall or designated point. A player who is captured goes over to the other team. During the game a player may change sides many times. The name he responds to depends upon which team he is on at the time.

The leader creates suspense not only by varying the order in which he calls either Crows or Cranes but also by drawing out the call, for example, "Crrrrooows," or by using the word in a conversational tone.

The game ends while the chase is still exciting. There is no winner.

DANCE FREEZE

A party novelty when there are facilities for dancing and music, this game brings everyone up on the floor. As in all true elimination games, it is fun to watch after being eliminated. Those who are eliminated may help out as judges. The success of *Dance Freeze* depends in part upon the ability of the leader, who serves as MC and also determines how long the music will play and what tempo it will be. This game is recommended for 10-year-olds and up.

Equipment
Piano and pianist or public address system with record player. Leader controls music by using volume control on record player. Leader also may sing if she can be heard.

Formation
Couples on floor as for ballroom dancing.

Action
The rules are simple. Everyone dances when the music is playing. Everyone stands motionless—freezes—when the music is not playing. The MC may give the dancers directions when the music is not playing, but no one must move. Either person moving eliminates the couple.

Once the music starts, the game is on. The MC has many tricks up her sleeve to trap the dancers. She does this by stopping the music suddenly, by changing tunes and tempo, by repartee designed to make someone laugh while the music is not playing, by instructing the group to dance when the music is off, by asking them to change partners while the music is playing and then, later, when it is off, saying "change partners" or "O.K., dance." This game affords the MC an excellent opportunity to exercise ingenuity.

The only rule stated at the beginning of the game is that participants move when there is music and not move when it is off. The last couple on the floor is the winner.

DIZZY LIZZY

Dizzy Lizzy is one of several relay games included in this book. As can be expected, it is an active game. The relays in this book, however, place less emphasis on running speed than do traditional relays and more emphasis on participation by everyone. Recommended for ages 8 and up.

Equipment
One baseball bat, or its equivalent, for each team.

Formation
Relay lines, each team with an equal number of players. Volunteers (one per team) serve as counters. Each counter holds a bat and stands facing the team, which is 20 to 40 feet away.

Action
At the signal, the first player in each team runs to the volunteer counter facing her. The player takes the bat, places her hands as a cushion on top of the bat, bends over, and rests her forehead on her hands with the other end of the bat touching the ground. She then circles the bat seven times, while the counter checks the number. (The number of times may be raised or lowered depending upon the age of the players.) The counter also makes sure that the player keeps her head on the bat and that the other end of the bat is touching the ground.

When the count is completed, the player releases the bat and usually staggers to her team, touching the next player in line. The first player then takes a place at the end of the line. This continues until each player has gone and the team is back in its starting order. The first team back in its starting order wins and should sit down.

Note
This relay should be played on a grassy area only. Advise the players in advance that if anyone has a problem with dizziness, this relay may not be for her.

DOTS AND LINES

Indoor   *2–3 Players*

Here is a game that can be enjoyed when there are only two or three
players or when others who are expected are slow in arriving. The game
can be taught quickly (especially if charts are prepared in advance), and
twosomes or threesomes can be scattered about the room. But do give
those who start playing time to finish the game before moving to another
game.

Equipment
Pencils and paper.

Formation
None.

Action
Pairs or trios of players prepare
their game chart. The chart consists
of ten rows of ten dots each.
(See illustration.) An X is drawn
through one dot in the top line,
eliminating it from being connected
to another dot.

　　　Each player in turn draws one
line connecting two dots. The
object of the game is for players to try to use their line on each turn to
complete a box. After completing a box, the player initials the box and
draws another line. Every time a box is completed, the player is entitled
to draw another line. The winner is the player with initials in the most
boxes.

DRAWING IN THE DARK

Indoor   *5 or More Players*

Take a dark room, or close your eyes, and you have all it takes for an
excellent warmer-upper. Teenagers, adults young and old, mixed-age
groups—all enjoy this one-shot novelty. The artist and the scribbler are
equals in the "dark."

Equipment
A sheet of blank paper, a pencil for each participant, and a firm surface
on which to draw.

Formation

Players sit around a table with paper and pencil before them. Classroom chairs with writing arms or any substitute may be used, even the floor, if players can draw on it.

Action

Players are instructed to place their pencils on the paper and to grasp the paper firmly so that all drawing will be on the paper once the lights are out or eyes are closed. Prior to turning out the lights, players are also told that they are to draw only what they are told, not to add embellishments. The lights will be turned on when the drawing is completed.

The lights are then turned off, and the leader directs the drawing of a house. It is important that the instructions be confusing, jumping from one part of the house to an object away from the house, for example: "Draw the outline of a house. . . . Now put a tree in the yard. . . . Oh, yes, there should be two windows in the house. . . . And a bird's nest in the tree. . . . Oh, I forgot, put a door between the two windows. . . . And there is a bird flying halfway between the house and the tree. . . . There is a chimney on the house, just a chimney. . . . There are three little birds in the nest with their beaks open, waiting to be fed. . . . And last but not least, there is smoke coming out of the chimney."

The above is one example. Use your inventiveness and make up your own drawing instructions if you wish.

After concluding the instructions, the leader turns on the lights or tells the group to open their eyes. Gasps of astonishment at what they have drawn will be followed by laughter as the players share their drawings with their neighbors. It is fun, conversation producing, and interesting to circulate the drawings. No one should feel uncomfortable or ill-at-ease, since all labored under the same handicap, and none has produced a "work of art." They have shared an enjoyable experience together in a relaxed fashion.

Note

This novelty cannot be repeated with the same group. Even with different instructions, the group will know the trick.

DZIEN DOBRY (POLISH)

Indoor or Outdoor   ***20–30 Players***

Suspense, laughter, and an element of vigor characterizes this game. Although a mixed-age group can play, the game will be most enjoyable for groups from 8 up that are matched physically. Two versions are offered in this book, one American and the other Polish. For the American version, see *Howdy, Neighbor*.

Equipment
None.

Formation
Players stand in a circle.

Action
One person volunteers to be "it" and walks around the outside of the circle. When "it" taps another player in the circle, he says, *"Dzien dobry"* ("good morning"). "It" continues in the direction he was walking, while the tapped player immediately begins walking around the outside of the circle in the opposite direction.

When the two players meet on the opposite side, they halt and say *"Jak sie masz"* ("how do you do") three times, bowing deeply each time. (*Jak sie masz* is pronounced "yock sheh mush.") Following this exchange, both players continue in the direction they were walking. The first one to reach the tapped player's place in the circle is safe, and the other one is "it."

An alternative to walking around the outside of the circle is for the two players to walk around the inside, close to the other players. This makes the two walkers more visible to the circle, but it is important to emphasize "no cutting corners" and "walk, don't run."

The leader should stress that *"dzien dobry"* and *"jak sie masz"* must be said loudly enough for all to hear.

If one player proves unequal to the task of beating another player more than twice in a row, the leader should switch the roles and make the other player "it."

Note
If a leader consistently protects all players against becoming unduly tired, the players will be accustomed to the practice and will not feel singled out. In games like *Three Deep* and *Elbow Tag*, it is useful to call "reverse," changing the person chased to "it," and "it" to the one chased.

ELBOW TAG

Indoor or Outdoor   *14–30 Players*

An exciting and fast-moving game where the emphasis is upon quick change of partners, *Elbow Tag* incorporates the same concepts as *Three Deep*. Don't mix the age groups too much on this one, although it is good for children, teenagers, and young adults. The mixture depends somewhat upon the group. Children in the 8–11 category sometimes have trouble with the idea of not being tagged, but action is speedy, and even they can be swept up in the spirit of the game.

Equipment
None.

Formation
A large open area is needed. Players pair up, hooking either right or left elbows so that they face in opposite directions. The pairs scatter randomly, but far enough apart for the runners to pass between two pairs and to "hook on" to a pair. Each player holds his free hand (the arm not hooked to his partner) on his hip, creating an opening for "hooking on."

Action
One player volunteers to be chased and a second player to chase him. When the chase starts, the two players run between the pairs until the chased player is safe. To be safe the chased player must hook his arm through a free elbow, facing in the opposite direction from the player with whom he hooks, *before* the chaser tags him. If he is tagged, the positions reverse. If he succeeds in hooking on, the player hooked on the other side starts running. The chaser now goes after him without pause.

   The object for the chaser is to tag the runner before he hooks on. The latter tries to hook on as speedily as he can.

   In teaching the game, the leader can say that its purpose is not to set up a race or endurance contest between two people but to get as many players into action as possible. This means speedy hooking on.

Note
The game can be boring for many of the pairs if a few people make a race out of the game while the others stand idly by and watch.

ELEPHANT AND GIRAFFE

Indoor or Outdoor   ***20–40 Players***

This game is excellent for adults, teenagers, and especially family groups, since all ages can participate together, down to the 5-year-olds. Don't take the game too seriously, but play it to the hilt for fast changing.

Equipment
None.

Formation
Players stand in a circle, close enough to reach their neighbors without straining.

Action
Once the game has been demonstrated and depending upon the number playing, the leader calls for three to six players to be "its" and to stand in the center of the circle.

Without taking a long time, each "it" points at a player standing in the circle and says either "elephant" or "giraffe." If the word is *elephant,* the player places both fists in front of her nose, while the players on her immediate right and left simultaneously cup a hand behind one of her ears. If "it" says "giraffe," the player raises both arms directly above her head, while her immediate neighbors shoot a hand straight toward her side. (The hand should be at a right angle to her body, and parallel to the floor. Do not be surprised if she jumps—especially if she's ticklish.)

Elephant

Giraffe

After naming the animal, "it" counts to 10. If the action is not completed in time by any or all of the three players, or if any of the three forgets or makes the wrong move, then "it" takes her place in the circle, and the player (or players) who made an error becomes "it." One "it" may make all three players miss, bringing three "its" in for one "it" going out. Don't worry. The more the merrier.

You will have to be your own judge on when to end.

EL TIGRE, LA PERSONA, Y LA CÁMARA (ARGENTINIAN)

Indoor or Outdoor   *20–40 Players*

In this game the ages can be mixed, starting as young as 6, and, if you're so inclined, boys can play against girls. All kinds of leaders will pop up as each group decides what it is going to do.

In Argentina this game is traditionally called *El Tigre, el Hombre, y el Fusil* (The Tiger, the Man, and the Gun). The version presented here substitutes "the person" for "the man," and "the camera" for "the gun" in order to be more in tune with current concerns. In this game, many adults and children will recognize the universal theme of *Rock, Scissor, Paper* (see Variations).

Equipment
None.

Formation
Players are divided into two teams. Each team goes to one side of the room.

Action
Each team decides whether it will represent a tiger, a person, or a camera. When both teams have agreed upon their action, they advance toward each other. On a signal from the leader (usually at the end of a count of three), every team member strikes the agreed-upon pose. A point is scored each time a team wins. If both teams strike the same pose, it is a draw—no score.

What wins: tiger wins over person (because it can eat the person); person wins over camera (because the person can operate the camera); and camera wins over tiger (because it can capture the tiger on film).

Poses
Tiger—arms raised over head, hands extended as claws.
Person—knees bent, arms extended to sides.
Camera—hands held in front of face as though snapping a camera.

Variations

An American version of this game is called *Rock, Scissor, Paper*. Instead of the expansive movements of the Argentine version, the moves are the following:

  Rock—right hand in fist.
  Scissor—right hand with second and third finger out, and
    other fingers closed in fist.
  Paper—right hand open, palm down.

Rock wins over scissor because it can break the scissor. Scissor wins over paper because it can cut paper. Paper wins over rock because it can hide rock.

An active version of both *El Tigre* and *Rock, Scissor, Paper* uses a safe area for each team to run back to. When the teams have decided what action they will take, they line up facing each other no more than 3 feet apart. On the count of three, the teams do their action (pose). Whichever team wins chases the losing players to their team's safe area (as in *Crows and Cranes*). All players tagged change sides. This is a win-win version.

A second win-win version is to divide into three or four teams. The teams do not have to be even in size. Each team again decides which of the three things it will do. When ready, the teams line up but do not advance toward each other. On the count of three they again do their action. The object this time is for all the teams to strike the same pose. The game is repeated until the object is achieved.

Note

Rock, Scissor, Paper is sometimes called *Rochambeau* in the West. In China it is called *Ching, Chang, Pock,* and in Japan it is called *Jan, Ken, Pon*. The same symbolism of rock, scissor, paper characterizes the Chinese and Japanese versions. In Japan *Jan, Ken, Pon* is played on trains, in the street, and in the home. In this book the game is used to choose who goes first in the Japanese game *Kendo*.

FACE TO FACE

Indoor or Outdoor   *20–40 Players*

This game is a good mixer, bringing players together through eye and physical contact. All age groups from 6 up can play.

Equipment

None.

Formation
Pairs of players scatter themselves around a room or within a designated area outdoors.

Action
One player, preferably an extra player, volunteers to be "it." When she calls "face to face," all players face their partners. On the command "back to back," they turn and stand back to back. When "it" calls "change," all players find another partner and resume the last-called position. In the scramble, "it" finds a partner, and the extra person becomes "it." The new "it" now calls the positions.

THE GAME

Indoor   *10–20 Players*
In this version of *The Game* participants do not have to act until they are ready. The reader will find in these directions an emphasis on dramatizing, not on signals. Without pressure for speed, there is no need for elaborate sign language. *The Game* is excellent for a group that has had some experience with simpler dramatic games (for example, *I'm Thinking of a Word That Rhymes With*). It is for all but the small fry.

Equipment
Chairs, benches, couches, sofas, or anything for sitting, including the floor.

Formation
Players sit in a semicircle.

Action

A player thinks of a slogan, a saying, a proverb, a song title, a book title, a poem title, the first line of a poem, or a word. Whatever it is, players should attempt to select a word or phrase with acting possibilities.

When a player has something in mind, she whispers it to anyone who volunteers to act it out. The clear space at the far side of the semicircle is a natural stage. As the volunteer acts, players try to guess what she is acting. The actor may not talk or make a sound, but she may nod her head or indicate with her hands if a player is hot or cold.

A few simple signs may be used to indicate what a player is acting.

1. The number of fingers held up indicates the number of words.
2. The number of fingers extended on wrist indicate which syllable is being acted.
3. Arms extended in a broad circular motion means the player is acting out the entire idea of the saying, not the individual words.
4. Arms extended and hands pushing toward the back indicates that the player is acting out background, or the setting. (For example, "revolt" and "guillotine" might be acted out to indicate the setting of the French Revolution for the phrase "Let them eat cake.")

Once the piece being acted out is guessed, the actor resumes her place in the circle. Another player volunteers something to be acted, and someone else offers to act it out.

Note

Players should not be expected to take turns. In games involving acting, there are always some players who are reluctant to act. By permitting players to volunteer to act out a word, the initiative is left to them. Before much time passes, most players will join in. Do not push the others. Sooner or later they, too, will act out a word, if you create a situation in which they can do this comfortably.

GUARD THE CHAIR

Indoor or Outdoor   *15–20 Players*

Here is an exciting version of dodgeball with little chance of a player being hurt by a thrown ball. And it will indeed be a nimble player who can successfully guard the chair for any length of time, especially as the team concept develops among the players in the circle. Players should be old enough to handle and throw a ball.

Equipment
A chair and a volleyball (not inflated too hard).

Formation
Players standing in a circle, not too close together, with the chair in the center.

Action
"It" has the job of guarding the chair from being hit by the ball. He cannot use his hands but can use any other part of his body.

Players in the circle may pass the ball to each other and, whenever they choose, throw the ball at the chair. If the chair is hit, the player throwing the ball becomes "it" and has the privilege of guarding the chair.

HANDS DOWN 54

Indoor or Outdoor   *10–15 Players*
Hands Down 54 has an interesting and somewhat tricky ritual to go through. Eight-year-olds and above can play.

Equipment
None.

Formation
Players stand in a circle. Each player's right hand is on top of the next player's left palm.

Action
One player starts the rhythm. She begins by saying "Hands down 54," followed by two claps. All players do the same thing in time with her. The chant is:

Hands down 54 *(clap, clap)*
On the list *(clap, clap)*
Names of . . . *(clap, clap)*

At this point the starting player names a category (such as flowers or countries) without breaking the rhythm.

One of each *(clap, clap)*
No repeats *(clap, clap)*
No hesitations *(clap, clap)*
So let's go *(clap, clap)*

Starting with the next player to the right, each player in turn names, without breaking the rhythm, something in the category: for example, rose, daffodil, and so on. Whenever someone breaks the rhythm, the player to her right starts it again, including naming the next category.

HOT POTATO

Indoor or Outdoor   *10–15 Players*
The element of keeping a person from touching an object has long characterized many games. In New York City, we called such a game *Saloogie*. Here *Saloogie* is combined with another element, the player's imagination. The imagination must see the object passed as being so "hot" that players cannot hold on to it long without burning their hands. Fun for 6-year-olds and up, but don't mix heights too much.

Equipment
A beanbag or a flimsy cloth.

Formation
Players stand in a close circle.

Action
"It" stands within the circle. The beanbag or cloth is tossed from one person to another. Each player, on receiving the "hot potato," calls out "hot potato" and quickly tosses it to another player. "It" tries to touch the

hot potato in flight or in a player's possession. Either way, if "it" succeeds in touching the hot potato, the player last touching it becomes "it."

Using a flimsy cloth instead of a beanbag makes the action more suspenseful since the hot potato will float through air, requiring speedy retrieval to keep "it" from touching the potato.

HOW DO YOU LIKE YOUR NEIGHBOR?

Indoor   *20–40 Players*

This game has many versions. One of the most common is *Fruit Basket.* The game lends itself to all ages and particularly to mixed-age and family groups. Everyone can play. One of the best "get-acquainted" games in any repertoire, *How Do You Like Your Neighbor?* offers ample opportunity for speedy movement, confusion, and physical contact—essential ingredients to assist the most inhibited in forgetting themselves and suddenly realizing they no longer feel strange in the group.

Equipment
Chairs without arms, one less than the number of players.

Formation
Players are seated in a large circle. The more space, the better.

Action
Players number off, including the player who is "it" (usually the leader). He stands in center of circle, points at a seated player, and asks him, "How do you like your neighbor?" If the player answers, "I like him," every player must get up quickly and find a different seat. In the scramble, "it" also finds a seat. The player left without a seat becomes "it."

An alternate answer to "How do you like your neighbor?" is "I don't like him." A second question must then be asked: "Whom would you rather have?" The player replies by naming any two numbers except his own. The individuals seated immediately on the right and left of him rise at once and attempt to change places with the two whose numbers were called. The player calling the numbers does not change his seat. Nor can the two neighbors exchange seats. They must change with the players whose numbers were called—unless one of the numbers called is that of the neighbor. In this case, he remains in his place.

In any event, "it" tries to get one of the four vacated seats while the neighbors and the two whose numbers were called scramble to change places.

Note
Persons sitting next to empty chairs should, to the extent possible, reach out and hold the chairs firm as players scramble to find seats.

HOWDY, NEIGHBOR

Indoor   *20–40 Players*

Suspense, laughter, and an element of vigor characterize this game. Although a mixed-age group can play, including children, the game will be most enjoyable for evenly matched groups. Two versions are offered in this book, one American and the other Polish. For the Polish version, see *Dzien Dobry*. This game is good for ages 7 and up.

Equipment
None.

Formation
Couples stand in a circle. Each couple holds nearest hands, separating itself from the couple on either side.

Action
One couple is "it." They walk counterclockwise around the inside of the circle, close to the other couples, until they tap one of the couples in the circle. Immediately the "it" couple speeds up, walking rapidly in the direction in which they were going (counterclockwise), while the tapped couple walks rapidly in the opposite direction (clockwise). Both couples must stay close to the circle and not cut corners or run.

When the two couples meet on the opposite side of the circle, they must stop, shake hands with the person facing them, and loudly say "Howdy, neighbor" three times. They then rejoin hands with their partners and continue to walk rapidly around the circle.

The couple who reaches the vacant place in the circle first wins; the losing couple is "it" for the next round.

Variation
Howdy, Neighbor can also be played outside the circle, although playing it inside best enables participants to see and hear what is happening.

HUMAN TIC TAC TOE

Indoor   *20–30 Players*

This is a quiet game for any age (except for those who are too young to know how to play Tic Tac Toe). The human element adds to the fun and opens the game to many more players. This game can be played with older adults, people in wheelchairs, and, in fact, anyone who can move about in any fashion.

Equipment
Nine chairs. If chairs are not available, lines indicating position can be drawn on the floor.

Formation
The players are divided into two teams, standing in lines facing the chairs. Three rows of three chairs are placed evenly in tic-tac-toe position. The first three chairs should be about 10 feet from the first person in each team.

Action
When taking their turn, the members of one team indicate O by placing both hands on the head. The other team is X and makes that sign by folding the arms across the chest. A team begins by having its first player select a chair, then sit in the chosen chair, facing the two teams while making his team's sign. He holds the sign until Tic Tac Toe is completed.

Then the first player on the other team goes, following the same procedure. The O and X teams continue to take turns. Each player determines for himself where he will sit.

As in paper *Tic Tac Toe*, the first team to complete a line horizontally, vertically, or diagonally through the playing field scores a point. A tie results in no score. The team with the most points wins.

All players in each scoring round retire to the end of their line when a point is scored. Players move up and start another round.

I'M THINKING OF A WORD THAT RHYMES WITH

Indoor   *15 to 25 Players*

A dramatic game that provides a relaxed introduction to the many forms of charades, including *The Game,* this one is good for all age groups and is especially good for mixed ages. With a little patience on the part of the adults, children can join in and may surprise the adults with their vocabularies. Recommended for ages 7 and up.

Equipment
Chairs or benches or the floor.

Formation
Players sit in a circle.

Action
"It" may begin the game by saying, "I'm thinking of a word that rhymes with *rat.*" The word she has in mind could be *fat* or any other one-syllable word that rhymes with *rat.* She must have a specific word in mind and must stick with that word until it is guessed.

As other players think of a word rhyming with *rat,* they raise a hand. When a player is acknowledged by "it," she acts out her word in pantomime. If "it" understands the action, she identifies the word and says, "*Cat?* No, it isn't *cat.*" If "it" cannot guess the word being acted but other players do, the other players check with the one doing the acting and then help her in dramatizing the word. The more the merrier. "It" must identify the word being acted before another player can introduce a different word that rhymes with *rat*. Caution all players that the only person to guess what word is being acted is the "it."

The object is for the players to act out the particular word "it" selected. When a player acts out that word, that player starts the game again with another one-syllable word. If several people are acting out the word when "it" guesses what they are doing, the person who started the action is next to be "it."

If a word has more than one meaning—for example, *bat* meaning a flying mammal and *bat* meaning baseball—both meanings eventually should be acted. Otherwise, "it" can wait until the meaning she has in mind is acted.

Note

Players should not be expected to take turns around the circle. In games involving acting there are always some players who are reluctant to act. Permitting players to volunteer to act out a word leaves the initiative to them. Before much time passes, most players in the circle will have joined in. Do not push the others. Sooner or later they, too, will act out a word, if you create a situation in which they can do this comfortably.

JUMP STICK RELAY

Indoor or Outdoor   ***14 or More Players***

Here is a relay requiring nimble feet, or a skinned shin will result. The game is good for single sex or coed groups of any age from 7 up as long as the players are physically agile.

Equipment

One broom handle or baseball bat per relay team.

Formation

Relay lines with an equal number of players in each team. A wall, a person, or a chair marks the spot to which the first person in each team runs. Distance varies, depending on age and physical ability.

Action

The first person in each team holds the "stick" at one end. On the signal "go," he runs the indicated distance, touches the wall (or goes around the chair or person), and returns to his team.

On reaching the team, the runner hands the other end of the stick to the next player in line. The two players bend down and hold the stick parallel to the ground at a height of about 6 inches. Then they go up the line of players, and each player in turn jumps over the stick. The stick must be firmly held by both players the entire time they run up the line. If a player steps on it or knocks it out of their hands, they must resume at that point in the line.

On reaching the end of the line, the first player remains there. The second player retains the stick and runs to the indicated point, returns, and offers the end of the stick to the next in line.

Each player takes a turn running. The line that is in its original order first wins.

KANGAROO RELAY

Indoor or Outdoor   ***14 or More Players***

Anyone who can hop with both feet and enjoy a relay in which the emphasis is not upon speed will like this one. So many relays emphasize racing that many children and adults, even though they may enjoy the exciting competition of a relay, have learned to shun them for fear of "slowing down the team."

Equipment

One volleyball per relay team. The volleyball should be slightly under-inflated.

Formation
Relay lines with an equal number of players in each team.

Action
The first player in each team holds the volleyball. At the signal "go," each player in turn hands the ball over his head to the next player. When the last player in line receives the ball, he places it between his knees, puts his hands on his hips, and hops kangaroo-style to the head of the line. He then passes the ball over his head. This action is repeated until the last person has gone and the team is back in its original order. The first team in order wins.

If the ball is dropped while being passed overhead, the player dropping it must recover it and resume passing at his place in line. If the "kangaroo" drops the ball while hopping, he picks it up and resumes hopping at the point where the ball was dropped. If the "kangaroo" takes his hands off his hips, the leader returns him to the point at which he removed his hands, and he continues from there.

KENDO (JAPANESE)

Indoor or Outdoor   *14 or More Players*
Kendo is played with great verve in Japan. It is one of several Japanese games that use the concept of taking a position different from that of the leader. If one takes the same position, one loses. "Kendo" is the name for Japanese-style fencing.

Equipment
None.

Formation

Pairs of players scatter around the playing area. Each pair stands one player behind the other. The player behind places both hands on the shoulders of the player in front.

Action

Pairs move about the playing area, meeting other pairs. When two pairs meet, the lead person in each pair plays *Jan, Ken, Pon* (see *El Tigre*) to determine who goes first (Illustration 1). Having determined this, the two lead players face each other, holding their fists clenched, one fist above the other (as though holding the Kendo sword—Illustration 2). The player who is to go first shouts "Keyaaa!" and then lunges forward, making one of three moves while shouting its name:

> *Men* (the face mask)—both hands, palms down, are placed on either side of the top of the player's head. (See Illustration 4.)
> *Do* (the chest plate)—both hands, palms in, are placed on either side of the abdomen, just above the groin. (See Illustration 3.)
> *Kote* (the arm guards)—the fingers of the right hand are placed on the left forearm. (See Illustrations 3 and 4.)

When the player lunges forward and makes the *Men* movement, he shouts *"Men."* As he makes the *Do* or *Kote* movement, he shouts *"Do"* or *"Kote"* accordingly.

The facing lead player simultaneously responds with a counter move, shouting the name of the move. If the move is different, the roles change, and the facing player initiates the action. This exchange continues until one of the two players makes the same response. This player loses and steps behind his partner.

The pair loses when both players lose. They then seek another pair, and *Jan, Ken, Pon* is played to determine who goes first. Preferably, pairs continue to seek new pairs with whom to play.

LAST COUPLE STOOP

Indoor or Outdoor   ***20–40 Players***

Excellent for teenagers, adults, and family groups, this is a true elimination game, one that is fun to watch and judge as well as to play (and sometimes safer). One go-around and this game generates real "do-or-die" spirit. It is advisable to mention ahead of time that it is rough.

Equipment

Enough indoor space to permit the formation of a double circle and a record player. If a record player is not available, the leader can sing.

Formation

Players pair up. Couples stand in double circle, creating inner and outer circle. Players on inside face in opposite direction from partners. One person, who isn't playing, serves as a judge.

Action

Players are advised to take a good look at their own partners and to remember them. When the music starts, each circle moves in the opposite direction. When the music or singing stops, players run directly to their partners. On reaching each other, partners take hold of both hands and squat.

The last couple to squat with both hands joined is eliminated and joins the judges in eliminating others.

It is often necessary to remind players to keep the circles large. The tendency is to make the circles smaller and smaller so one can be closer to one's partner. If playing with more than 15 pairs, it is not necessary to play until one couple is left. Declare the last three to five couples the winners.

LEMME STICKS (TITI-TORIA—MAORI)

Indoor or Outdoor   *2 Players*

Lemme Sticks (sometimes called *Lummi Sticks*), a Maori (New Zealand) stick game, intrigues and challenges adults and children alike, from the youngest to the oldest. All you have to be able to do is to sit cross-legged on the floor or, at the least, squat with the assistance of a backrest like a wall, a tree, or another player.

Once you master the figures described below, try the game with four players seated facing each other. Sticks fly across the square in rhythm in amazing defiance of what should be an inevitable collision. Just be sure that one pair of players starts three beats after the other.

Equipment
Four lemme sticks for every two players. The stick is 18" long and approximately 1" in diameter. Old broom handles or dowels can be cut for use.

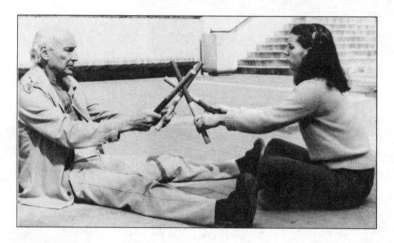

Formation
Two players face each other, sitting cross-legged on the floor or ground. They must be close enough so that they can easily toss the sticks to each other. There should be no more than 1 foot between the players' hands when their arms are extended.

As many pairs as wish to play can be scattered around the area. Each pair sings the song for itself, although for teaching purposes, it is advisable to have all pairs learn in unison.

Music

Ma ku ay Ko ta o We ku e Tan o

Ma ku ay Ko ta o We ku e Tan o

Action

Hold the sticks perpendicular to the ground, about one-third of the way up. When tossing sticks to your partner, try to throw with a slight upward as well as a forward thrust, keeping the sticks perpendicular to the ground.

In synchronization with the rhythm of the song, the following figures are beaten out, stick against ground, and stick against stick.

Tap the Sticks

1   (a) Holding the sticks vertically in front of you, tap the lower ends on the ground.
    (b) Tap the two sticks together.
    (c) Then tap your right stick against your partner's right stick.
    (d) Repeat 1(a), (b), and (c), but tap your left stick against your partner's left stick.

2   (a) Repeat 1(a) and (b).
    (b) Tap your right stick against your partner's right stick, and your left stick against your partner's left stick without pausing.
    (c) Repeat 2(a) and (b).

3   (a) Repeat 1(a) and (b).
    (b) Tap both sticks against your partner's sticks. Agree in advance who will tap from outside in and who will tap from inside out.
    (c) Repeat 3(a) and (b).

Toss the Stick

4   Repeat figures 1 through 3, but toss the sticks to your partner instead of tapping the sticks. When tossing both sticks at once, agree who tosses on the inside and who tosses on the outside.

Toss the Sticks in Square

5   (a) Holding the sticks vertically, tap the lower ends on the ground, tap the two sticks together, and then toss the stick in your left hand to your right hand while simultaneously tossing the stick in your right hand to your partner's left hand.
    (b) Repeat this square pattern for the remainder of the music.

Flip the Sticks

6   (a) Holding your right stick extended to the right side, tap the far end of the stick on the ground, flip the stick, catching it at the opposite end, and tap the far end again.
    (b) Repeat 6(a), but with your left stick.

(c) Holding both sticks parallel to the ground in front of you, tap the far ends on the ground, flip the sticks, and tap the far end again.

(d) Holding both sticks vertically, tap the lower ends on the ground, hit your sticks against each other, then toss the stick in your right hand to your partner's right hand, while your partner tosses the stick in his right hand to your right hand.

(e) Repeat (a) through (d), but players start with left stick and end by tossing their left stick to their partner's left hand.

7 (a) Holding both sticks parallel to the ground to your sides, tap the ground with the ends farthest from you, flip the sticks as in 6(a), catch the sticks, and tap the far ends again on the ground.

(b) Holding both sticks parallel to the ground in front of you, tap the ground with the far ends, flip the sticks in a circle, catch them, and tap the far ends again on the ground.

(c) Holding both sticks vertically, tap the ground with the lower ends, tap the sticks against each other, then toss the stick in your right hand to your partner's right hand, while your partner tosses the stick in his right hand to your right hand.

(d) Repeat (c), but players toss their left stick to their partner's left hand.

(e) Repeat (a) through (d).

Note
Each figure is repeated for one complete singing of the chant. Each figure, if correctly done, is completed at the end of a chant.

LICENSE PLATE

In a Car   *2–4 Players*
This game is fun on car trips when conversation languishes and scenery no longer occupies the travelers' attention. Those with fairly extensive vocabularies have the advantage.

Equipment
A car in transit.

Formation
None.

Action

As players spy combinations of successive letters on the license plates of passing cars, a rider calls out the letters. Each rider tries to come up quickly with a word including that combination of letters. The combination of letters can be separated: for example, BLE—*bale* or *bowled*. The rider coming up with *bale* would win that round because she added the fewest letters.

MAGIC MUSIC

Indoor or Outdoor   *10–20 Players*

Players are always surprised at how much a person can be cued to do just by indicating whether the player is "hot" or "cold." In this game there is the added element of group singing. The recommended age is 6 and up.

Equipment

None, or chairs.

Formation

Players seated in a circle on the ground or on chairs.

Action

"It" volunteers to go out of the room or far enough from the circle not to hear what the group decides he should do.

The players select a specific action for "it" to perform when he returns to the circle, for example, remove the right shoe from a particular player, and give it to another particular player.

The players also select a well-known song and begin singing it at moderate volume. When "it" hears the singing, he returns and enters the circle.

Players in the circle sing louder when "it" is hot and softer when "it" is cold. When "it" successfully guesses and completes the action, another player volunteers to go out.

MUSICAL CHAIRS

Indoor   **_10–20 Players_**

This little-used version of _Musical Chairs_ incorporates an element of problem solving to make it more exciting. Since it is considerably more active than the usual way of playing, children (age 8 or over) and teenagers love it. Adults and families enjoy it, too.

Equipment
A chair for all but one of the players.

Formation
Chairs without arms are arranged next to each other in a straight line, alternately facing in opposite directions. Players stand by chairs, prepared to walk in counter-clockwise direction.

Action
If piano or record player is available, music is played to cue the players when to walk. If not, the leader sings. In either case, when music or singing is heard, the players walk. When the music or singing stops, the players rush to the nearest empty seat.

Since there is one less seat than players, one player will be left standing after the scramble and be eliminated. However, instead of eliminating a chair and the player as is customary, the eliminated player chooses a chair in the line and sits in it. All other players stand and resume walking when the music starts.

Each time another eliminated player chooses a chair, the remaining players have to run farther and search harder to find an empty seat. Those who have been eliminated stay in the game and share in the excitement of those trying to avoid elimination. It is usually necessary to urge players to keep moving and not tarry by the empty seats.

NAME BALL (TEAM JUGGLE)

Outdoor or Indoor   ***10–20 Players***

Many games include passing a ball and the use of players' names.
Although no time pressure is placed on a player to remember another's
name, this game does require remembering players' names. The addition
of more balls makes the game more complicated and even more lively.

Equipment
2 to 6 lightweight balls. Half must be a different size, color, or pattern.

Formation
Players stand in a circle with space to permit catching and throwing a ball
in any direction.

Action
Each player learns the first name of the player on his left and on his right.
A lead player then names the person on his right and tosses one of the
balls (henceforth designated as the "forward ball") to that player. The ball
is passed consecutively around the circle as each thrower names the
person to whom he throws. The ball may be passed around the circle two
or three times, so that people become familiar with each other's names.
Players should remember the name of the person from whom the ball
comes and the name of the person to whom they pass it.

Players then scramble around to different positions in the circle. Any
player with the "forward ball" locates the person who was on his right,
names him, and tosses the ball to him. That player in turn does the same
thing with the player who was on his right. Should a player miss for any
reason, another player may pick the ball up and resume play.

When the passing is well along, a second ball (which looks different)
can be passed to the person who normally gives the player the forward
ball. This ball is called a "reverse ball."

Once the game is well under way, additional forward and reverse
balls may be used. Players can be asked to change places more than
once.

OJIISAN-OBAASAN (JAPANESE)

Indoor or Outdoor   ***15–25 Players***

There is no better evidence of the international character of games than this Japanese version of the blindfold game *Reuben and Rachel*. In Japan *ojiisan* is "grandfather" and *obaasan* is "grandmother." Children from age 7, teenagers, and adults can play this game, but don't mix the age groups.

Equipment
Two blindfolds and a gong-type bell.

Formation
Players form a circle, standing close enough together to keep the *ojiisan* and the *obaasan* inside its boundaries but allowing sufficient room for the two to maneuver about.

Action
If the two volunteers are of the opposite sex, their identification as *ojiisan* and *obaasan* is obvious. If they are of the same sex, arbitrarily assign the names.

"Obaasan, Obaasan"

One player is blindfolded. (The game can also be played with both players blindfolded.) The other player holds the bell. Turn the blindfolded player around two or three times. He calls the opposite player, *"obaasan, obaasan."* Every time he calls, *obaasan* must jingle the bell.

The object is for the blindfolded player to locate the sound and touch the other player. The player who is not blindfolded attempts to evade him but cannot leave the circle and must always ring the bell as soon as her name is called.

When the first player has succeeded, the second player is blindfolded, and the action is repeated, with the second player calling *"ojiisan, ojiisan."*

PLATE, POTATO, BROOM RELAY (GERMAN)

Indoor or Outdoor   *14–30 Players*

This relay is enjoyable whether you watch it or take part. Recommended for ages 8 and up.

Equipment

For each team, a chair, a potato, a whisk broom with strings attached, and an unbreakable dinner plate.

Formation

Players line up in relay formation, preferably no more than eight to a team. Chairs are placed at one end of the room. The relay teams line up, facing the chairs, at a distance of about 25 feet.

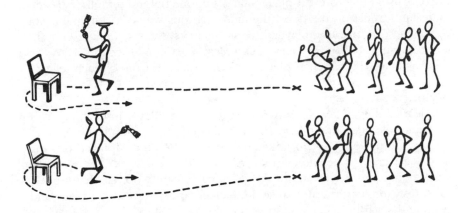

Action

Before seeking volunteers, the leader explains and demonstrates what the players will do.

The first player in each team receives a plate, a potato, and a broom. He must place the potato between his knees, balance the plate on his head, and twirl the whisk broom by its string by placing it over his index finger. Thus balancing the three objects, he must walk, shuffle, or otherwise locomote to the chair in front of his team, go around it, and return to his team. If any object is dropped, the player retrieves the object, replaces it, and resumes at the point where it was dropped. The next player then takes the objects and repeats the activity.

The first team back in its original position is the winner.

PLAY PARTY RELAY

Indoor   ***15–20 Players***

This game is a sure-fire, vigorous relay for most ages, if the player can recognize a tune and is fairly agile. It is fun to play and almost as much fun to watch. Use this relay during a break between other activities, when you want to offer something for the very energetic while permitting others to relax. Or use it to include everybody.

Equipment

A piano, accordion, or other melody-producing instrument and someone to play it. Or the leader can sing.

Formation

Relay team of five to eight players lines up, one behind the other. Teams may stand, squat on the floor (the most vigorous way of playing and not recommended for older players), or sit in chairs (there is danger of a chair overturning when player races back unless a teammate secures it). A point is marked (or a chair placed) about 20 feet in front of each team.

Action

The leader assigns a well-known song to the first player in each team. For example, the first person in each team may be given "Skip to My Lou," the second player "Captain Jinks," and so on. The tune is played or sung as it is assigned to be sure all players know it.

When a tune is played, the player in each team who has that tune must rise, run forward and around the chair, and return to her place and resume the starting position (squatting, sitting, or standing). The first player back in her place scores a point for her team.

The musician (or singer) calls the turn by playing (or singing) the tunes in varying order. A few impartial judges will be needed to determine accurately who has gotten back to her place first.

Note

Play Party songs or singing games were popular with the early settlers and pioneers. Other Play Party games in this book are *Bingo* and *Rig-a-Jig-Jig*.

POLITE CONVERSATION

A party novelty, this game has even enjoyed brief popularity on TV. Use this game when people are relaxed and ready to enjoy someone else's conversational ability. Nine-year-olds and up will enjoy the game as long as the two contestants are more or less evenly matched. Before calling for volunteers, be sure to advise players that the game places a premium upon conversational ability.

Equipment
Chairs, benches, or the floor.

Formation
Players are seated in a circle, although only two people play at a time.

Action
While the two volunteers are out of earshot, the group chooses two completely dissimilar sentences. The sentences should not relate to a natural interest of the player. For example, a player might be given "The area of a circle is pi r^2," while the other could have "The Pilgrims landed at Plymouth Rock in 1620."

The players return, one at a time. Each is secretly given his sentence. Each is told he must insert his sentence in the conversation exactly as he got it.

The two players sit down facing each other and begin to converse. They must carry on their conversation without pauses, must be polite and listen to each other without interrupting, and must respond to questions asked. One person may not monopolize the conversation. Each player attempts to include in the conversation the exact sentence he has been given. This must be done so that it passes undetected by the other player.

If a player thinks he knows when the other has said his sentence and what it is, he may challenge the player and state the sentence. If he is correct, he is the winner. If he is incorrect, he has used one of three challenges. Three unsuccessful challenges lose the game for the challenger.

A player wins when he has succeeded in inserting his sentence without challenge, and the conversation has continued.

The fun in this game arises out of the efforts of each contestant to steer the conversation in the appropriate direction for the inclusion of his sentence. Remember to explain the game before recruiting two volunteers.

POSTURE TAG

Indoor or Outdoor   ***15–25 Players***

One of the many versions of tag, this game adds the novelty of moving while balancing a beanbag on one's head—hence the title. This game is recommended for ages 8 and up.

Equipment

Two rectangular, loosely filled beanbags (preferably about 6" x 3"). The bags should be flexible enough to mold to the top of a player's head.

Formation

Players scatter themselves about the playing area.

Action

Two players volunteer, one to be "it" and the other to be chased. Each places a beanbag on top of her head. The player being chased becomes "safe" by placing her bag on another player's head. The latter may assist in the process. The two active players may not hold the beanbag on their heads.

If the beanbag is successfully placed on another player's head, then "it" chases that person. Whenever "it" tags the other player, that player becomes "it" and chases the one who tagged her.

If the beanbag falls off the head of the player being chased, that player automatically becomes "it," and the roles are reversed. If the beanbag falls off the head of "it," that player picks it up and continues as "it."

THE PRETZEL

Description will not suffice. This game has to be played to find out what it is like. The game places players in close contact and is best played when group members are very comfortable with one another. This game is recommended for 7-year-olds and up.

Equipment
None.

Formation
Circles of eight to ten players. Each circle constitutes a separate "pretzel."

Action
One player from each circle volunteers to untwist the pretzel after it is formed. He leaves the room so he does not see the pretzel being formed.

The remaining players in the circle, without dropping joined hands, maneuver themselves into a twisted mass of humanity. This is done by lifting arms over heads, by stepping over another player's arms, going between a player's legs, ducking under another's arms, and so on. The ingenuity of the players will provide far more methods for creating new convolutions than can be outlined here.

As players maneuver themselves into position, the circle is inevitably drawn closer together into a tight knot of people with hands and arms protruding all over the place. The player who volunteered to untwist the pretzel returns and physically moves players in the circle until he has restored the group to its original circle formation. He must be careful not to cause a player to drop hands with his neighbor.

Those finishing first can offer advice to other pretzels. The hilarity of untangling is the major focus of the game.

PROOI (DUTCH)

Indoor   *15–40 Players*

This Dutch version of the American game *Sardine* has the advantage of keeping the group all together within one room—and can be hilarious. It is best played by a group whose members have already reached the point of being comfortable with one another. All ages can play together (except the youngest ones, below the age of 6).

Equipment
None.

Formation

None. The game requires a room large enough for the players to move about freely but not so large that they roam too far. It must be possible to darken the room by turning out the lights. If not, eyes may be kept closed until a player is with the *prooi*.

Action

One player is the *prooi* (pronounced "proy"). No one knows who she is. The lights are turned out, and all players begin moving around the room in the dark, hands outstretched.

The players move about constantly. When a player bumps into or encounters another, she asks, *"Prooi?"* When the *prooi* is asked this question, she takes hold of the player's hand, whereupon that player also becomes silent and does not respond when touched by another player still seeking the *prooi*. When the player touched is not the *prooi,* she must immediately answer by repeating, *"prooi,"* and both players continue moving about in search of the *prooi*.

Gradually, as more and more players locate the *prooi*, they huddle in one group with the *prooi,* all holding hands with one another. The room becomes increasingly silent as fewer and fewer players continue the search.

The game ends when all players have found the *prooi* or when the leader thinks it has gone on long enough.

PROVERBS

Indoor or Outdoor   ***10–20 Players***

Most of the words in any proverb are common ones, but a few are not. This game can be a real challenge to the player who has to try to conceal one of those words in a few sentences. The game is recommended for ages 10 and up.

Equipment

Chairs, or players can sit on the floor or the ground.

Formation

Players sit in a circle.

Action

One player volunteers to be "it." After "it" leaves the room or goes out of earshot, the players in the circle decide on a proverb, for example, "A stitch in time saves nine." Each player in turn receives one of the proverb's words in the order that the words occur in the proverb. Words can be distributed to either the right or the left.

Players are told that their task will be to incorporate their word unobtrusively into the answers they give to questions "it" will ask. At the same time, players are cautioned not to talk on and on.

"It" returns to the circle and, starting anywhere, asks a player a question. He may ask more than one question of the same player, go from one player to the next, or skip players. Through his questions, "it" tries to pick out the word of the proverb concealed in each player's responses. When he guesses the proverb, another player volunteers to be "it."

Variation

Players must incorporate their word in one sentence.

QUICK LINE-UP

Indoor or Outdoor   *20 or More Players*

All ages from 8 up enjoy this vigorous game. Each age group can play at its own speed. A real body-contact mixer, the game combines elements of movement, confusion, and guessing.

Equipment

None.

Formation

The space needed depends upon the number of people playing. A gym, a dance floor, or a large game room will do. This game can be played outdoors also. Players are divided into four teams, with each team forming one side of a square. All teams must be equidistant from the leader who stands in the center. Each team has its players standing in order of height, with the shortest player on the right and the tallest on the left.

Action

The leader faces Team 1. Team 2 is to his left. Team 3 faces his back. Team 4 is on his right. Each team must always be in this order with respect to the leader.

Two or three judges are needed. Judges should stand on chairs or a bench to be able to see which team is in position first. Since the teams must be equal in number, if there are two to three extra players, they can be judges.

The leader pivots in place, being careful not to reveal in what position she will end up. As soon as she completes turning and faces one team, all teams race to gain their proper position, lining up in order of height as outlined above. The first team to line up in the proper order and in the right place in relation to the leader scores a point.

Team members must move individually; they are not permitted to hold hands as they move. Judges should not assume that the team whose hands are up first are properly in place. Players frequently find themselves in the wrong line or on the wrong end of the line.

After several rounds, the leader may elect to move anywhere in the room or on the field. Teams must follow and reassemble as above.

REVERSE BUZZ

Indoor or Outdoor   *15–25 Players*

Buzz-Fizz-Buzz and *Fizz-Boom-Buzz* are but a couple of the variations that many people know for this fascinating game with numbers. Few appear to know *Reverse Buzz.* As in most mental games, this is a quiet game.

The goal is for the group to reach the count of 50 without making an error. Eliminating an individual who makes a mistake, as the game is frequently played, has the natural result of losing that player's interest and reducing the game to a contest of wits between those who are the most nimble with numbers.

Equipment

Chairs or benches help but are not essential. Players can sit on the floor or ground.

Formation
Players sit in a circle.

Action
The leader begins counting by saying "One." The player to his left says "Two," and so on round the circle. Whenever a player has to say a number with 7 in it (for example, 17), or a number that can be divided by 7 (for example 21), he must say "buzz" instead.

When a player says "buzz," the player to his right—not his left—resumes the count with the next number. This is the reverse element. The player who said "buzz" then continues with the count as before. If the player to the right has a number that also calls for a "buzz," the play continues to reverse back one more player to the right before resuming with normal progression to the left.

A player who fails to say "buzz" when he should or says a number or "buzz" out of turn must start the process all over again with the number 1.

The game ends when the group reaches 50 without an error.

RIG-A-JIG-JIG

Indoor   ***20 or More Players***
A simple game good for everyone, *Rig-a-Jig-Jig* has the added value that it starts with no partners and ends with couples. This attribute is not only useful in pairing people off when group members are still strangers, but is also especially good for teenagers and that difficult 12–14 age group.

Equipment
None, although a piano and piano player come in handy.

Formation
Circle with no partners. One person is inside the circle. The dance needs a large room or gym, depending upon the number of dancers. The leader and group can sing the song.

Music

1st Verse:

As I was walking down the street,   down the street. As
down the street,

I was walking down the street, heigh-ho, heigh - ho, heigh-ho!

Chorus:

Rig-a - jig -jig and a- way we go, a - way we go, a - way we go.

Rig-a - jig - jig and a -way we go, heigh-ho, heigh-ho, heigh-ho!

2nd Verse:

> A pretty girl I chanced to meet,
> Chanced to meet, chanced to meet.
> A pretty girl I chanced to meet,
> Heigh-ho, heigh-ho, heigh-ho.

Action

During the first verse, the circle walks counterclockwise, while the extra person walks clockwise, close to the circle.

During the second verse, the circle goes clockwise, and the extra person goes counterclockwise. He selects a partner of the opposite sex before the verse ends. (It is sometimes desirable with a particularly young group to omit choosing partners of the opposite sex.) During the chorus, the circle stands still, while the extra person and his partner, hands joined in skating position (arms crossed with right hand holding right hand, and left hand holding left hand), skip around the inside of the circle.

At the end of the verse he places his partner in front of him, single file. As the dance repeats, the two walk clockwise inside the circle, and the circle moves counterclockwise. During the third verse, both people choose partners from the circle.

This process repeats until almost all players are inside, at which point it is time for the next game or dance to start—preferably a game or dance that takes advantage of the fact that the group is paired off.

Note
Games such as this one (and *Bingo* and *Play Party Relay*), known as "Play Party games," were popular with the early settlers and pioneers.

SARDINE

Indoor or Outdoor   *10–20 Players*
This is a quiet game. Suspense builds as player after player disappears from sight. Families, teenagers, and children 6 and up—all but the older adults—enjoy *Sardine*.

Equipment
None.

Formation
If you play outdoors, use terrain with clearly established boundaries beyond which the game is not to go. Within the boundaries there must be hideaways large enough to accommodate all the players at one time. If you play indoors, closets, attics, and other nooks serve as hiding places.

Action
One player is the sardine. While all other players hide their eyes and count to 100, the sardine finds a place in which to hide. The hiding spot must be large enough to permit all the other players to join the sardine and still not be seen.

After counting to 100, players scatter and independently seek to find the sardine's hiding place. When a player finds the spot, she unobtrusively enters and becomes one of those hiding from the rest of the players. She does not have to enter as soon as she discovers the place. (Do not teach this point. Let the group find out.)

When all but one player are hidden or in the "sardine can," the game ends, and the remaining player is "it" for the next round.

SCAVENGER HUNT

Indoor or Outdoor   ***20 or More Players***

Another sure-fire game for large groups. This one is not vigorous. The game—a version of the more complex and lengthier *Scavenger Hunt,* in which teams are given lists of items to accumulate that may require their ranging far afield—can be played in any fair-sized room and does not require that the players leave the room. It is a good mixer, develops quick and ready participation, and can be used at any time, while a group is still "cold" or after the ice has been broken by several other activities. Six-year-olds on through teens and older adults as well as families all find this game fun.

Equipment
None.

Formation
Divide the group into teams. The number of teams and their size depends upon the number playing and the amount of space. Teams are dispersed so that each one is distinct and approximately equidistant from the leader.

Action
Each team sends one player to the leader. The leader names an item of clothing, something that a person might be carrying or have in a pocket or purse, or some other article that might be somewhere in the room (such as a shoelace, a ring, a shirt, a comb, a book, a nickel). As soon as the players know what item they are to get, they simultaneously race back to their teams and ask for the article. The player reporting to the leader cannot offer an item of her own if she has it. She and her teammates can get the item anywhere. They are not limited to possessions of members of their team.

Once the article is produced or found by any member of the team, the player who had gone out originally takes it and runs back to the leader. The first person back to the leader with the article scores a point for her team.

SCRAMBLED ANATOMY
(THIS IS MY NOSE)

Indoor or Outdoor   *10–15 Players*

Do you know which is your elbow and which is your nose? Sure, but maybe not when you have only to the count of 10 to do the opposite of someone who says, "This is my nose," and points to his elbow. Try this game with a relatively small group. The confusion leads to laughter. Eight-year-olds and up can play.

Equipment
None.

Formation
Players stand in a circle. One player volunteers to be "it." If there are more than 15 players, two or more people can be "it."

Action
Facing a player in the circle, "it" touches a part of his own body, but calls it another part of his body. For example, he says, "This is my nose," as he touches his elbow.

"It" then counts to 10. Before the count is completed, the other player is expected to touch his nose and say, "This is my elbow."

If the player fails to perform the action within the count of 10, he becomes "it." If he succeeds, "it" goes on to another player.

THE SLAVES OF JOB (CANADIAN)

Indoor or Outdoor   *5–10 Players*

As with many "passing-the-shoe" games, this one is universal. An American shoe-passing game uses a song, "You must pass this shoe from me to you, to you. You must pass this shoe and *do just what I do.*" The italicized words call for the same back-and-forth movement by the players holding a shoe as does "zig-a zig-a zag" in *The Slaves of Job.* Recently, I learned a French version sung to the same tune as the American version. The words are:

Savez-vous passer ce traderidia?

Savez-vous passer ceci sans vous trômper?

In any event, this shoe-passing game is fun for any age. Six-year-olds on up through adults will find the game challenging. The almost inevitable pile-up of shoes adds to the merriment.

The Slaves of Job were playing catch and go. They'd

take it and leave it and take it a-gain. While

playing they'd go zig - a zig - a zig - a zig - a zag.

Equipment
Shoes.

Formation
Players sit or kneel in a circle on the floor. Each contributes one shoe to the game.

Action
Each player sings the song and, with her right hand, places a shoe in front of the person on the right every other beat: "The *slaves* of *Job* were *playing catch* and *go*." The shoe is passed on the italicized word or syllable. On the alternate beat another shoe is picked up from the left.

Continue passing shoes in the same manner until "*zig-a zig-a zig-a zig-a zag*." Then each player holds on to the shoe and beats time on the italicized syllable, alternating between right and left hand. On *"zag"* the player releases the shoe to the right.

Variation
It is sometimes fun to do the game the first time with singing, the second time with humming, and the third time with all players singing silently to themselves.

SNATCH THE BACON

Indoor or Outdoor   *14–30 Players*

This is a semi-active game with opportunities for developing many strategies. Do not be disappointed if it takes a while for players to begin to develop the strategies. It is fun when played either with a pell-mell rush or more carefully. *Snatch the Bacon* can be played equally well indoors or outdoors as long as the playing area is large enough. Most ages, including families, will enjoy this game.

Equipment
A handkerchief, keys on a ring, or any small object that can be "snatched."

Formation
Two teams line up facing each other, about 20 to 30 feet apart. When the game is played indoors, a line should be drawn clearly for each team. Similarly, when the game is played outdoors, each team's position should be clearly indicated. Teams arrange themselves by height, with the shortest person on the right-hand end of the line and the tallest on the left.

Action
Each team numbers off, starting at the right-hand end of the line. The "bacon" is placed midway between the teams.

The leader, who is not playing, calls a number. Both players with that number run to the center to "snatch the bacon."

The player who reaches the bacon first picks it up, turns, and tries to run back to his place in line before being tagged by the other player. If he gets there without being tagged, he scores two points for his side. If the other player tags him before he reaches his place, a point is scored for the other team. If a player touches the bacon without picking it up, a point is scored for the other side. The team with the highest score at the end of the game wins.

The leader should call every number at least once and can call some numbers more than once.

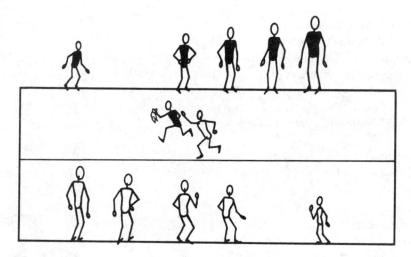

Variations

1. The leader can call two to three numbers at the same time.
2. If there is not already a visible midline, the leader can draw a short line midway between the teams and place the bacon on the line. Neither player is permitted to step on or over the line when his number is called until a player actually picks up the bacon. If a player steps over or touches the line before the bacon is snatched, a point is scored for the other side, and the players retire to their respective places.

SPOKE TAG

This vigorous game is fun for everyone. It is sure-fire if the group is in approximately the same age range. Whether the group is coed or single sex makes no difference. However, the game should only be played outdoors on a grassy area. The players should not be wearing good clothes, because the least that may happen to them will be grass stains. Nine-year-olds and up can play.

Equipment
None.

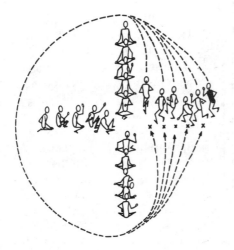

Formation
Depending upon the number of players, divide the group into three or four teams. Each team lines up. The teams position themselves like the spokes of a wheel, with each team facing the hub. Then all squat on the ground. The players at the head of each spoke sit close together facing each other to make the hub. There should be enough space for running around outside the spokes.

Action
One person is "it" and walks around the outside of the spokes. Without undue delay, "it" taps the last person in one of the spokes. The player who is tapped rises, then taps the shoulder of the player seated ahead of her. Each player in turn repeats this procedure until the entire team, or "spoke," is standing.

The player at the hub of the spoke, when she is ready, runs to either the right or the left. All players must run in the same direction, including "it." No one runs until the player at the hub has started. All players must run around the outside of the other spokes until they get back to their own spoke's position. Players cannot jump over seated players.

The object is to get around quickly and resume a seated position in your spoke. If you can outrun the player at the hub, you gain that position and will determine the direction the next time round. The last player back, who will be seated at the end of the spoke, is "it" for the next round.

SQUARE RELAY

Here is one for everybody. The game is especially good for families, since all ages from 6 up can participate. In ten seconds flat, each team will be rooting like mad in a frenzy of excitement. Easy to get going, this game can be played at any point and is good when a group is still in the getting-acquainted stage.

Equipment

Each player should have a chair without arms (benches can be used if necessary), an extra chair, and four coins or small objects.

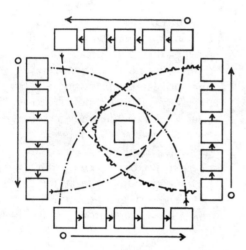

Formation

The group is divided into four teams. Each player takes a chair and sets it up in a line with his team, parallel to one of the walls, so that all players on the team face the center of the room. The four teams are thus arranged in a square formation. Be careful that the corners do not touch. Make sure that each player's chair is close to the next player's and that each team's chairs are in a straight line.

One chair is placed in the center of the room, equidistant from each line of chairs.

Action

Each player on the left-hand end of his team is handed a small object, for example, a key, a coin, or a small beanbag. The objects should be identical for each team.

At the signal "go," the object is passed along the line, with each player passing it in turn to the player on his right. Each must handle the object. If it is dropped, the player dropping it retrieves it and continues.

As soon as the player at the end of the line receives the object, he rises, runs around the center chair without touching it, and runs back to the beginning (left-hand end) of his line. Simultaneously, everybody in the line moves right one seat so that the seat on the left end is vacant. The runner takes the vacant end seat and starts the object moving to the right again.

The relay is repeated until the members of the team are back in their original positions. The first team back in its original position scores a point.

The number of times the relay is played depends largely on the group's enthusiasm and age. Three or four times is generally enough.

STEAL THE DOG'S BONE

Indoor or Outdoor   ***15–25 Players***
Old and young alike will respond to this challenge. And if you need a game to quiet a noisy group, this will do it. Be sure the circle is large enough to permit adequate space for the player to sneak to the center from the circle. Six-year-olds and up can play.

Equipment
Any small object can serve as a bone, such as a beanbag, a small stick, or keys (which make the "bone" somewhat more difficult to steal). A handkerchief or scarf for a blindfold is also needed. Chairs are optional.

Formation
Players are seated in a circle. The "dog," or "it," squats on the floor in the center of the circle. The "bone" is placed close to her after she is blindfolded.

Action
A player who indicates her desire to try to steal the bone is silently chosen by the leader. All other players remain perfectly quiet. (This game cannot be played with other activities going on within earshot or nonplayers talking or walking about.) The thief rises and attempts to reach the bone, take it, and return to her place without being heard. If "it" hears a noise, she points in the direction of the sound and says, "Bow-

wow." She may do this every time she hears a noise. If she points in the direction of the player who is trying to steal the bone, the player must retire to her seat without the bone. If she is pointed at after getting the bone but before sitting down in her place, she must give the bone back to the leader who places it near the dog again.

Only one player at a time may attempt to steal the bone. Other players should not make noise to distract the dog. The dog does not remove her blindfold until the bone is successfully stolen. She is told in advance that the leader will let her know when the bone is stolen. Players cannot walk around the outside of the circle prior to moving in to steal the bone. The dog cannot sweep her arm around but must point in one direction at a time.

When playing with young children, try to give everyone a chance, but do not hesitate to permit some players to go more than once. Otherwise, the children will perceive that they will not have another chance until all others have taken a turn, and they may become restless.

SWAT

Indoor   ***10–20 Players***

Speedy action and suspense characterize this game. Make sure to have sturdy chairs without arms and one or two extra people to steady the empty chairs. Do not mix the ages too much in this one. If you do, the kids will have it all over the older players.

Equipment

A chair for each player, a stool (preferably a piano stool or piano bench) for the middle of the circle, and a "swat"—a foam bat or a roll of newspaper secured with cellophane tape or masking tape. Do not use too many sheets of newspaper, just enough to provide firmness so that the "swat" will not fall apart when used. Due to wear and tear, it is advisable to have two swats on hand.

Formation

Players sit in a large circle, with piano stool in the center.

Action

"It" has the swat. He leaves his seat and walks around the inside of the circle, deciding whom he will swat below the knees. As soon as "it" swats a player, he runs to the center, places the swat upon the piano stool, and races back to his own seat. Meanwhile, the player swatted chases "it" to the piano stool, picks up the swat, and attempts to swat "it" before he can reach his seat.

If "it" succeeds in reaching his seat, the other player becomes the new "it" and starts the play over again. If the original "it" is hit before sitting down in his seat, the player with the swat turns and puts the swat back on the stool in the center and tries to regain his seat before "it" can swat him.

Quite a seesaw can take place in this game, and it may be occasionally necessary for the leader to halt the back-and-forth and designate another "it" before a player is too exhausted.

Another important rule, and one that creates considerable suspense and mirth, is that the swat must be placed on the stool. If it falls off the stool, the player who put it on the stool must return and pick it up. The player doing the chasing simply waits at the stool for the swat to be replaced.

Players should be cautioned not to take too long deciding whom to swat. The fun of the game is action, not deliberation. Deliberation is particularly a problem with younger players. A little encouragement and example-setting by the leader will quickly overcome it.

Note

Since players race back to their seats and jump into them with considerable force, it is advisable to have someone who is not playing stand in back of each empty seat as a backstop to prevent the chair and player from toppling over backward.

THREE DEEP

This is another version of the tag games in which one member of a pair must run when a third person joins the pair. (See *Elbow Tag* and *Bronco Tag*.) *Three Deep* is a vigorous game for those who are "it" or being chased. But problem solving in this one adds to the fun and lessens the strenuous nature of the game.

Equipment
None.

Formation
Pairs of players stand facing the center in two concentric circles, with one person right behind the other. The pairs should be far enough apart, however, so that other players can run between them.

Action
One player volunteers to be "it," and a second player volunteers to be chased. Chasing must be done only around the circle, not inside it.

The person being chased achieves safety when she runs directly in front of a pair of players and stands there. (She cannot run in front of more than one pair.) The pair now is "three deep," and the outside person (on the outer edge of the circle) must run. "It" now chases that person.

The object is for "it" to tag the runner before that person runs in front of a pair and is safe. If a runner is so tagged, she turns and chases the tagger, who now must run in front of a pair to be safe.

At times the leader may call "reverse," if an exhausting seesaw takes place between "it" and the "runner."

TWO-WAY GHOST

Indoor or Outdoor   *5–10 Players*

Ghost is an old favorite for the many situations when a quiet game is in order. Adding the element of "two-way" makes it more challenging and offers greater opportunity for ingenuity. Teenagers and adults, whether they have played the simpler version or not, enjoy *Two-way Ghost.* (Younger groups can play *Ghost.* Its directions also appear below.)

Equipment
None.

Formation
Players sit in a circle on chairs or on the ground.

Action
The group agrees on the minimum length of a word that, when completed, gives the person finishing the word a letter of the word *ghost.* Four- or five-letter minimums are usually long enough.

In *Ghost,* one player begins by naming any letter of the alphabet. In turn, each player to his left adds another letter. When adding a letter, the player is expected to have a specific word in mind. If the player following him cannot think of a word or does not believe the other has a word in mind, he can challenge him. If the challenge is successful and no word was in mind, the player who added the last letter receives a letter in the word *ghost.*

In *Two-way Ghost* a player can place his letter either before or after what has already been given. For example, three players have gone and the letters are *a, r,* and *f,* in that order. The next player might add *c* before the *a,* building toward *scarf.* In order to make this clear, each player repeats all the letters, including his own, in the correct order, so that all know where the letter has been added.

Letters can be added only before or after what has been given. No letter can be inserted between the letters already given.

The game is normally over when one person in the game has acquired *g, h, o, s,* and *t.* If interest is still strong and the players wish to continue, the player who has all the letters of *ghost* no longer gets a turn to name the first letter but can attempt to add a letter when his turn comes or get other players to talk to him. If the next player accepts a letter from him or talks to him, he also gets a letter in the word *ghost.*

UP JENKINS (HANDS UP)

Indoor   *10–20 Players*

No matter which name you prefer for this game, it is loads of fun. My favorite time and place to play it is after holiday dinners, when everyone is replete with food and conversation has dwindled, yet no one really wants to leave the table. Of course, the table must be rectangular (not circular), and there have to be enough present to constitute two sides.

Equipment
Chairs and a stone, coin, bean, or other object that can be easily passed and concealed in one's hand.

Formation
One line of players sits in chairs facing another line of players in chairs. The lines should not be farther than 4 feet apart. If the game is played at a dining table, the table separates the two lines of players.

Action
The player at the right-hand end of each line is the captain. The object to be passed is started by the captain of one team. All players on the team passing the object keep their hands behind their backs as they pass it. Hands move back and forth constantly with the object going from one player to another. The object can move in any direction. It does not have to go first to one end of the line before it goes the other way.

On the command "Up Jenkins" by the captain of the other team, the players passing the object hold their clenched hands above their heads. On the command "Down Jenkins," they place their hands, open with palms down, on their knees (or on the table).

Players on the opposing team, when they wish to guess, ask permission of their captain. When permission is given, the player must identify specifically which hand she wants turned over.

Players continue guessing until the hand concealing the object is turned over. Once the object is uncovered, a count is made of the number of hands turned up. That count becomes the score for the team trying to discover the object.

The second team now passes the object behind their backs and the process repeats.

The winning team is the team uncovering the least number of hands in locating the object.

Note

If played at a table, the object can be passed from hand to hand under the table.

Variation

A friend of mine who played this game with her family in the Amish country of Pennsylvania scores in exactly the opposite way. For her family the object was to avoid discovering the hand concealing the object. The winning team therefore was the team turning up the most hands.

WAVE THE OCEAN

Indoor   *15–25 Players*

Here is a game that depends upon the verve with which the players throw themselves into the situation. It is generally sure-fire, although it can lay an egg if used before group members have relaxed with each other. Eight-year-olds and up can play.

Equipment

Chairs without arms.

Formation

Players sit in tight circle, with no space between the chairs.

Action

"It" leaves his chair and stands in the center of the circle. When he directs the circle to "wave right," the player with the empty chair on his right moves into it. One at a time, each player quickly moves down a seat, trying to prevent "it" from sitting down. "It" may change the direction by saying, "Wave left." Then the players shift seats in the other direction.

"It" keeps trying to sit in an empty seat. If he succeeds, the player who should have moved into the empty chair becomes "it."

Players keep moving quickly down a seat until the direction is changed. The circle cannot move as a group. Only one player moves at a time.

WHEN I GO TO CALIFORNIA

Indoor   *5–10 Players*

This version of a memory game combines an element of acting. Young and old and those in between will enjoy the quiet challenge of this game, namely, to find out how many times the group can go round the circle before calling it quits. Eight-year-olds and up can play.

Equipment
Chairs, benches, couches, or the floor—anything for players to sit on.

Formation
Players sit in a circle.

Action
The first player rises and begins by saying, "When I go to California, I will take," and names an object that she will take, for example, a toothbrush. At the same time she acts out brushing her teeth.

The player to her left picks up by saying, "When I go to California, I will take my toothbrush [acting out brushing teeth as did the previous player] and my . . ." She adds another item and acts it out.

Each player, in turn, repeats and acts all that has gone before in the order in which it occurred and adds her own item.

If a player forgets an item or does one out of order, she does not add to the list on that turn. However, the next time around she has a chance to repeat what has gone before and add her own.

Variation
Items can be named without the acting element.